BEAVER ~TALES~

Audrey Tournay
and the
Aspen Valley
Beavers

AUDREY TOURNAY

The BOSTON
MILLS PRESS

A BOSTON MILLS PRESS BOOK

Published by Boston Mills Press, 2003
132 Main Street, Erin, Ontario N0B 1T0
Tel: 519-833-2407   Fax: 519-833-2195
e-mail: books@bostonmillspress.com
www.bostonmillspress.com

In Canada:
Distributed by Firefly Books Ltd.
3680 Victoria Park Avenue
Toronto, Ontario M2H 3K1

In the United States:
Distributed by Firefly Books (U.S.) Inc.
P.O. Box 1338, Ellicott Station
Buffalo, New York 14205

National Library of Canada Cataloguing in Publication

Tournay, Audrey, 1930-
Beaver tales : Audrey Tournay and the Aspen Valley beavers / Audrey Tournay.

ISBN 1-55046-410-8 (pbk.) — ISBN 1-55046-418-3 (bound).

1. Beavers. 2. Wildlife rehabilitation — Ontario — Parry Sound Region.
3. Beavers — Reintroduction — Ontario — Parry Sound Region.
4. Tournay, Audrey, 1930–. I. Title.

QL737.R632T69 2003   599.37   C2003-901187-9

Design by Gillian Stead
Printed in Canada

Dedicated

to the memory of

Cody

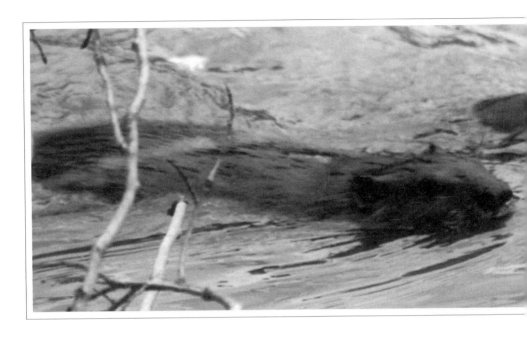

Contents

Beginnings

1

INTRODUCTION

If a forest can rejoice, and I think it can, that rejoicing will take place when a beaver selects a place on a stream or in a bay, builds a dam and a lodge and establishes residence. A pond will form, water weeds will grow, and habitat for all sorts of creatures will result — ducks, deer, moose, muskrats, raccoons, skunks, fish, frogs and dragonflies. The water will seep deep into the earth and nurture trees and plants, even during droughts. Beavers are basic to a healthy wilderness.

Over the years, I have known many beavers. Some have come to the Sanctuary as very small kits, orphaned and cold and hungry. Some have come as adults, injured, often angry. Mine has been the privilege of giving them the care they have required, and then, in most cases, returning them to the wild where they can live free, natural lives. These are the experiences I would like to share with you.

Aspen Valley Wildlife Sanctuary began many years ago; the beginning was unplanned. Its growth has been the result of a real need for a place of refuge for orphaned and injured wildlife.

All those years ago, I was walking my dogs down a small dirt road in Muskoka. The road wound uphill and down, through woods, across a little brook, uphill again and down. Through a break in the trees I saw a huge old gray barn, and the valley, a log house, and rail fences —

all very beautiful and very quiet. To the east, an arm of high rocks and tall pines edged the valley, to the south, a swamp and woods and hills, to the west and north more hills and rocks and woods. The great gray barn seemed to brood over the deserted house and the meadows around it. I remember especially the beauty and the stillness.

A year later, 1972, my dogs and I were living in that quiet valley. Some things had changed. The old log house had burned, but on the fieldstone foundation another small house stood sturdily, ready for the adventures that were to come. The barn, still strong after almost one hundred years, was the home of two horses and a goat named Bramble. The fence rails surrounded a large meadow where the horses grazed and, when being inside the fence suited her, Bramble. Though I was still teaching high school, life in the valley was satisfying. Predictable. Brimming with hours of walking and riding, drawing and reading. Rather wonderful.

And then the telephone rang. Over the years, the ringing of the telephone would come to signal the beginning of yet one more adventure. That first time, the conservation officer (a friend) asked simply, "I've got this orphaned raccoon. Want it?"

"Yes." I had no idea how that one-word answer would change life in the valley — would change my life. It was the beginning of the Sanctuary.

The valley is still beautiful. The two horses and the goat have long since died of old age. Other dogs play where the first two lived out their lives. And now other creatures stay here: raccoons, skunks, foxes, woodchucks, muskrats, beavers, deer, moose, bears, coyotes and wolves — even a cougar and a lynx — because their natural life has been interfered with, usually by human actions, and they have needed help. As long as an animal is in need of food or medical attention or simply time to grow, it stays with us; however, once it can be independent, we take it to a carefully chosen release site and return it to the free life it wants to live.

The Aspen Valley Wildlife Sanctuary is situated just outside the village of Rosseau (located at the northern tip of the Muskoka Lakes), a small, pleasant village founded over one hundred years ago. During the years, all sorts of creatures have spent their early babyhood in a warm container beside my wood stove. Bear cubs have slept there and raccoons and skunks and foxes and fawns. But above all, beavers!

In this vocation, one shouldn't have a favorite animal, for each requires lots of love, attention and understanding. And I will spend equal amounts of energy and time on any animal who needs it. But I cannot help, or really explain it. I love beavers!

Before I had much experience with wildlife, I earnestly believed that biologists were almost as inspired as Holy scripture. So, when I held that first tiny beaver in my hands and felt the warmth of life in its urgent body, I was almost frightened. I realized that I knew little about sustaining that life, fulfilling all its needs, or preparing it for its return to the wild. That return had been for me the end towards which I worked for every raccoon and skunk, deer or fox — now, any wild creature. But a beaver I did not know, so I turned to the biologists.

"What must I do to prepare him for living free?" I asked a government biologist. "What food? What living arrangements? What contact with humans?" But the biologist seemed to find my enthusiasm somewhat boring, my questions irrelevant. I showed him the little pond in our valley, where I hoped to be able to teach the beaver . . . what?

The biologist shrugged his shoulders. "It can't be done," he said. "He can't go free. Can't be done." Knowing what I know now about the official attitude towards beavers, I'm sure he was adding silently, "And doesn't need to be done."

Receiving no help there and watching the enthusiasm for life that the beaver kit continued to show, I turned to a friend who had a university degree in biology. "I want him to go free," I insisted. But again came the answer, "Can't be done. I had one once. Gave it to a zoo."

"Why can't it be done?" I knew the raccoons and the skunks, the deer and the foxes had all survived after they had been released.

"Family animal. Learns everything from its family," was the reply.

It seemed logical. I believed him. I would have to be his family, and that's the only excuse I have for keeping the first beavers I raised.

I held the little kit, living in a straw-filled kennel next to the warmth of the wood stove in my house. I helped him as he enthusiastically suckled his formula from the baby bottle, gripped in both his small hands, and I promised, "I will do the very best I can for you."

So began my long friendship with beavers. As I watched those first beavers, who did not go free, I saw intelligent animals, innovative, improvising with anything available in a household to do the work they would have done if they were free in a wetland. And the question grew and grew in my mind, "Why can't they go free? Why not?" Now, many years later, I can go out to various wetlands and watch beavers living wonderfully free lives, successful, fulfilled — beavers who grew up here at the Sanctuary and who have been set free.

Though I did not understand enough to give those first beavers their freedom, I do believe they lived full and good lives. And from them I learned, and many other adults and children have learned, just how wonderful beavers are.

As a nation, we flaunt the beaver as our symbol. Is the beaver our symbol because it's intelligent and industrious, contributing more than any other creature to our environment? No. It's our symbol because the search for its valuable hide led explorers across a continent. Our country was explored at the cost of the lives of millions and millions of beavers. As a child being taught the history of Canada, I thought of fur traders as noble, brave men in huge canoes, pushing farther and farther inland, trading with willing Native people and returning with loads of furs. Now, whenever I hear of fur traders, all I can think of is dead beavers.

For well over thirty years now I have lived with wild creatures. With many of them I have enjoyed friendship. And yet, for reasons I cannot in any way explain, I have learned to appreciate and (to some extent) understand the beaver above all others. I want to tell these stories of friendship to you, beginning with the first beavers with whom I shared my life completely, learning about them and from them. I also want to share my somewhat gradual realization that beavers do not have to be kept captive, not in my home and not in yours, and certainly not in a zoo. Even orphaned as a tiny kit, a beaver can grow up to swim away into the wilderness — and live.

Has our official attitude to the beaver changed? What have our governments done to protect beavers and their habitat? This year I went to the local Ministry of Natural Resources office and asked for a copy of the most recent legislation regarding beavers. All the person in charge could give me was a book entitled *The Beaver in Ontario*, published in 1972 and revised in 1976. Here, I learned that the chief importance of the beaver is purely economic — how many jobs, how much money it contributes to the human race. Even more alarming, on page twenty it was noted that "the Fish and Game Act provides that a private landowner may destroy beaver by any means at any time of year if beaver are causing damage to his property."

Damage? We once had a complaint from a cottager: "The beavers are eating my daisies!" It is legal to shoot beavers, to pour gasoline on the beaver lodges and burn them, and to dynamite them. And from these legal situations, we have received orphaned kits, burned, sick, frightened and very, very much alone.

Though the trade in furs persists, and humans still wear the skins of dead animals for fashion, fur commerce is no longer the only threat to the beaver. In Muskoka, the part of Ontario in which I live, beaver habitat is steadily diminishing. Huge homes line our lakes, and beautiful gardens are carefully cultivated as though they were city parks. Our lakes are sliced with racing boats. Golf courses take over the

13

once-quiet homes of wild things. The spring complaint of returning cottagers (also heard dozens of times during the summer!) recurs, as we answer our telephone to hear plaintive wails of, "There is a beaver in my boathouse!" or "The beavers are eating my trees!"

Whose trees? Whose lakes? I want to say, "If you don't like it, go back to the city!" But of course that would not be economically feasible. The government will recommend hiring a trapper or having the beaver shot. "Relocation," says the biologist, "doesn't work." But it does.

The phone rings often, too often, about the increasing numbers of orphaned or injured wildlife creatures. Because governments have done little to make the lives of wildlife better; because people have so little understanding of the benefits of beavers; and because help must be given to these, our fellow creatures, wildlife sanctuaries like the Aspen Valley Wildlife Sanctuary have become important. Yet sanctuaries have difficulties meeting the need. Without any kind of government support, they must depend entirely on the generosity of concerned, compassionate people for gifts of food, money, volunteer time and work.

If people think they're having problems with beavers, we can show them how to restrict beaver entry to their boathouses with chicken wire and also how to protect the trees. We can supply simple patterns for beaver bafflers to control water levels. Still, when I answer that complaint call and listen to the whining about "bad beavers," and the question, "What can I do?" I want to answer: "Enjoy them!"

Habitats are stressed. Pollution is causing problems, not only for the beavers but for all of our wildlife. Blind raccoons are now common, and blind skunks. This year we have a blind fawn. Last winter, a blind beaver was found wandering down a street in Bracebridge. And although these problems may be the result of genetic defects or illness, pollution in the environment also becomes suspect. A little porcupine, who did well at first and who had started to walk with a tilt, finally died from the same symptoms that had become evident in two little beaver kits. Autopsy results showed parasites in their brains caused from polluted water. We have also had foxes with deformed legs come into the Sanctuary.

For many of these, humans are responsible.

FORESHADOWING

This afternoon, when searching through my files for something I have yet to find, I came across some papers so old that they are almost beginning to yellow. As I read them, I began to remember and to wonder how I could have forgotten even a small story about a beaver. But memory of Ah-mik returned only partially, so I am glad I wrote about him almost thirty years ago, way back when the wonders of a Muskoka springtime were still new, and when Rosseau was a little village, not really discovered yet by tourists. The Sanctuary was, then, unimagined.

Duffy was a raccoon who had been given to me to take care of, simply because a friend knew that I liked raccoons. His presence in the story enables me to date my account of this early experience with a beaver. The year was 1972. Duffy had come into my life because he had broken his leg. I remember that because he thumped around the house like a drummer with no rhythm — difficult to forget! The memory of Ah-mik, quiet and simply passing through, was somehow buried beneath the tales of hundreds of other creatures. However, here it is.

May is a soft, green month. The woods burst into unbelievable life, each leaf uncurling, soft, succulent, green-gold. Rock cliffs shine with running water, and streams and little waterfalls flourish suddenly in unexpected places until all the woodland life is lived against a background of gurgling, splashing water. One listens for, and finally hears, the first frogs at night. Though frost often rims the ponds and water buckets in the early morning, the dawn becomes a chorus of birdsong. Nothing disturbs this Eden — until the blackflies move in to welcome the cottagers back!

All winter, the General Store has been a sleepy sort of place, where one can make the necessary purchases, meet one's neighbors and talk awhile. For about one hundred years the store has stood at the main intersection in the village, and during the decades it has changed little: food, overalls, milk and axes. Old pictures of the store show the gas lamps dangling over the heads of the slow-moving, gossiping locals. One picture shows a team of oxen standing outside, and Pauline Johnston, the poet who used to come here for her vacations, sitting, legs dangling, on the ox cart. Now the store has changed; it is as busy as a city supermarket, and there is little time for gossip. However, that May day in 1972, as I was checking out, the proprietor said to me, "Have they phoned you about the beaver yet?"

They had not. People waited in line while she explained, "Some young people who have a cottage down the lake found it on the road. They think it was hit by a car. I told them to take it out to you."

Knowing it would be only a matter of time before the phone rang, I drove slowly home, meditating on the possible complications of raising a beaver. As I drew up to the door the call came; one long ring, one short. I answered, and a young man's voice said, "We have a beaver we've been looking after, but we have to go back to the city. Will you take it?"

Of course.

Two heavily bearded, barefoot, kindly young men brought Ah-mik (the Ojibway word for beaver) to the farm. She lay lethargically in their arms, although apparently not injured anywhere. For a wild animal to accept human handling so meekly, something had to be wrong.

The day before this I had presented the veterinarian with Duffy, the raccoon with the broken leg, and on this day he accepted our return, even with a beaver, calmly enough. An Ontario Provincial Police officer, sitting in the waiting room, blinked somewhat and managed a polite, "That is a beaver, isn't it?"

It was a smallish beaver, so I could hold it easily covered in a blanket in my arms, only the dangling tail betraying its identity.

"Yes," I agreed. "It is a beaver."

Still doubting, "Does it bite?"

"No," I replied. But there had to be a reason why it did not.

Dr. Alan Christie laid the beaver on the table, turned on the bright overhead examination light and went over it carefully. His verdict: a concussion was making him so docile, and also a broken jaw.

We had to leave Ah-mik at the hospital for a few days after Dr. Christie wired the jaw. The beaver was put in a cage near Duffy (who had just had his broken leg set and was still slumbering, his leg in a cast). Their neighborly lives should have begun there, but no bond ever developed! Before Duffy, Ah-mik was home again, and our record book shows the pattern of the days following.

May 6, 1972: It has been snowing all night and most of the day; great, white, wet flakes have covered the ground, the fences and the roofs, and have made the yellow daffodils on the lawn droop in utter dejection. It is easy to think that this is just a continuation of the long winter and to forget the few weeks of spring that we had already had and that the grass beneath the snow is very, very green. It is not easy for me to comprehend the fact that at present a beaver is walking up and down the hallway of my house, pausing to sleep for an hour curled up by the organ, and then rousing himself to plod ponderously around Joey (the German Shepherd) and over anything else, up the hall, detouring into the bathroom (where sleep may overtake him again for an hour or so) and then on into my bedroom, where he curls up under the easel to rest from his great excursion and to gather energy for a return trip. No animal could be more of an opposite to Duffy, who can make the same circuit in half a minute flat without the idea of sleep ever occurring to him.

When I brought Ah-mik home last Thursday, I was given instructions that he must not be given the slightest chance to escape until the wire is removed from his jaw, a matter of at least ten days. I have fixed a cage for him down in the shallow part of the creek, and I leave him there part of every day. I think he needs the mud and the moisture. He does not think he needs the confinement. Therefore, the remainder of the time he is in the house, wandering around and exercising — or sleeping.

I had never thought of the beaver as a particularly beautiful animal, so the fact that Ah-Mik was so lovely surprised me. He weighed around twenty pounds but was bulky and awkward to carry. His coat was a luxurious, glimmering chestnut, rich, vital and unbelievably alive. His nose was very large, round and soft as velvet; and his eyes were small and black and regarded the world very gravely. His tail was flat (perhaps because he was still young) but not too heavy. His hind feet were very, very large and long, webbed and powerful. His front feet had no webs and were considerably smaller. All feet had five long toes, the center three much longer than the toes at the outer edges. His claws looked almost like human fingernails! When he sat up, he flipped his tail under so that he was sitting on it, almost as though it were a little rocking chair. That tail, seemingly quite a nuisance to him on land, trailed behind him uselessly so that when he turned a corner he had to give it an extra flip to make it follow him. His ears were small, soft and black, curled like tiny flower petals deep in his fur.

Ah-mik's introduction to civilization had been too violent for him really to enjoy people. He accepted food from us — lettuce, Triscuits, some dog kibble, tomatoes — and we gathered aspen branches. But with his jaw wired, he seemed to find chewing them difficult; we would find only strips of them eaten off. Once in a while he would seek company, pausing by my chair or bed and dozing awhile. But mostly he preferred his own private wandering. The bathtub held his attention longest.

I tried my best for him, bringing in various water weeds and putting them into the tub, filling it with water and leaving him there. Sometimes, if I wanted a bath, the removal of the beaver and all his furnishings was irksome, but mostly I managed. When he wanted out of the tub, he would have to struggle against the slippery sides until I came by and lifted him out. To dry him off was impossible — I had to let him waddle away, like a walking waterfall, and follow behind with a sponge. Once in a long while he chirred, perhaps with contentment. As he poured water throughout the house, I chirred a little too, but for a different reason!

My record book details my main concern regarding the beaver:

What his future is, I do not know. I have a feeling that, quite unlike Duffy, he will want to return to the wild. Since beaver do travel, even if we release him here in the valley he could move off in any direction and be in danger of traps. I do not want to send him to a zoo. I will talk to the Conservation Office about him to see if we can release him in Algonquin Park. There must be a safe place somewhere in this country for an amiable beaver.

Then Duffy returned from the veterinary clinic — joyously. He held no animosity towards the beaver that had invaded his house but swung happily around on three legs, holding his cast high off the ground.

Instead of letting him wander the wilds at night, we caged him. He was indignant, but we did not want whatever had injured him to renew the attack before he was ready to defend himself. Had he been consulted, of course, he would have insisted he was ready for any adventure.

In the house, Duffy was willing to acknowledge that the beaver was a very interesting creature. If he found Ah-mik asleep, he would sit on his haunches and begin poking at him, here and there, slowly, until the beaver would become annoyed, wake up, smack his tail on the floor and rumble away. But like fate, Duffy would follow. Once in a while, it seemed he had a distinct urge to play doctor, and he would pull at the wire in the beaver's jaw and twist it. The beaver never bit him, though. (I suspect it was because he could not move fast enough.) Eventually, Duffy would decide that a beaver was the dullest of all animals and swing away on his three legs to find a horse or a dog or a goat to torment, or to inspect the stream to see if he could find an early frog.

Because the veterinarian's office is near the school where I was teaching, twenty-five miles from the valley, I often had to take animals needing attention to school with me. The students, with enough maturity so that the class routine was not upset, soon learned to accept the presence of these creatures. When the day came that the wire was to be removed from Ah-mik's jaw, he had to come to school with me. He reacted to the art room with the same bored indifference he had bestowed on the house, plodding aimlessly among the easels, painting desks, and ceramic tables, under etching presses and over anything stacked on the floor. The students, accepting his presence, stepped aside as he plodded by. Once, an entire biology class dropped in for a visit. Since trapping is common in this area, many of the class had seen a dead beaver; however, few had had the privilege of touching and examining a live beaver. They were impressed, as I had been, by the gleaming beauty of the living animal, and Ah-mik was patient.

Ah-mik's patience continued, unruffled, when I took him to the veterinarian's office to have the pins removed, an operation that was quick and looked rather simple. The wires, like long, slender nails, were merely pulled out. As they were removed, Ah-mik shook his head and recommenced his slow, purposeful plod around the office.

Wires removed, Ah-mik was ready for release, and he broke out of his cage down at the creek. Wherever he finally went, I can imagine him plodding on and on. I was relieved that he left the way he had, as we had not been able to locate one place in all the area, not even Algonquin Park, where he would have been safe from trappers.

Still, thirty years later, no safe place exists.

A Few of the Beavers I Have Known

2

SWAMPY, THE FIRST SANCTUARY BEAVER

Years ago, when I entertained human company in my little house, most people were patient about my lack of housekeeping ability. They rather enjoyed the idea that a box of tiny raccoons or squirrels, even skunks (if tiny enough), might be close to the warmth of the wood stove, and they enjoyed the process of bottle feeding each hungry mouth. However, the charm of wildlife in the house generally vanished when the guest was confronted by a good-sized, not necessarily friendly beaver.

"Your bathroom," said a somewhat irate guest emerging from that room, "is an absolute mess!"

I didn't need to be told. I love the warm sterility of other people's bathrooms. With frankly acknowledged envy, I leaf through magazines and see soft white rugs, gleaming mirrors, and spotless tubs. I dream about luxurious baths in perfumed opulence, about climbing out of the fragrance and feeling my feet sink into the deep pile of the bath mat. However, a beaver lives here.

A beaver knows exactly how a bathroom should look. Towels should not hang on towel racks, they should be scrunched in piles (preferably soggy from

The doorstep was not made for baby beavers.

23

being dragged through a water dish) in the corner. Empty food dishes, carried from the kitchen, should be stashed behind the toilet. A small bundle of aspen sticks can be pushed into the linen shelves, or shredded and strewn over the soggy towels. Most delightful to the beaver, though, is newspaper. Newspapers can be pushed, pulled, crunched, wadded into water bowls, tucked behind pipes, and hidden (wet) in the vanity.

Eventually, of course, I was faced with a choice: guests or beavers? Beavers.

The events that can change an entire way of life often come unexpectedly, as they did with the beavers, and I still vividly remember that first call.

"Yes?"

"We have a small animal," said the conservation officer. "Found it beside the highway. Thought you might like it."

I waited. Raccoon? Fox? Squirrel?

"Little beaver," he said, "maybe a week or two old."

"Yes!" With one word and not even a slight hesitation, I had committed myself to years and years of fascinating friendships.

In the parking lot at the junction of Highways 69 and 141, I met the conservation officer. I took the kit from his hands and knew a moment of pure delight. In the midst of all the highway noise, I held a tiny part of the vast, quiet wilderness in my hands. The beaver whimpered softly. He was dark and soft, his little eyes black, shining and bewildered.

Though every Canadian recognizes a beaver — round and brown with a big flat tail; a proud, aggressive animal, the symbol of our country — in my hands was a frightened orphan, his tail a small gray paddle, his family dead.

I took the beaver home, made him a warm, towel-filled box with hot-water bottles, and when he seemed comfortable, fed him goat's milk from a baby bottle. He drank eagerly, snuggling against the hot-

Swampy in the pond.

water bottle. For a moment he was quiet, and then he began to whimper. Father? Mother? Siblings? To sleep alone was completely unnatural. So I picked him up, and in my arms, snoring gently, he slept. He needed the assurance of life around him. No baby beaver is meant to be alone.

I broke all the rules of wild-animal rehabilitation — I took him to bed with me. Tight against me, he slept, small and warm. During the night he wiggled his way under the blankets, right down to my feet. And then I learned one meaning of beaver pond!

Today, our enclosures for wildlife are out in the meadows and woods of the valley; in those days, some of the smallest orphans were cared for in the house with my dogs and me. The dogs were gentle Labs. One in particular, Kate, enjoyed mothering raccoons, skunks, or almost any creature who needed her. One skunk (de-scented by a previous owner) was making his home on the bottom shelf of the vanity. His name, with an exceptional lack of imagination, was Skunky. The beaver's name might have become Beaver, had not some children with slightly larger imaginations named him Swampy. Still, until other beavers arrived, I continued to call him Beaver. At the time, a raccoon kit named Snowman completed our household.

Back then I understood the hazards of having wild creatures indoors, the necessary care, and the ultimate goal — freedom. At least I thought I understood, until the beaver arrived.

Beavers have an important place in myth and legend, not only in North America but in northern countries around the world. As I watched Swampy growing, I began to understand some of the early beliefs about beavers, beliefs that set the beaver apart from all other animals except possibly bears and coyotes. Beavers, one west-coast myth claims, were originally a branch of the human race. They could talk with us freely, live with us, and interact on an equal level. However, being independent creatures, they were not necessarily obedient to the commands of the Creator (after all, beavers are exceptional creatures. They know it, and they assume the rest of creation knows it!). And so, the myth goes, until such time as the beavers reformed and gave, with no argument, complete obedience to the Creator, it became necessary to deprive them of their ability to speak and to make them wear fur. However, beavers being what they are, they will never obey anyone, and despite God's punishment, they have made a very good life for themselves. So I'm not sure who won that contest!

At any rate, Swampy took over our entire establishment. He trundled around the house as though it were his. At first he had a kennel beside the wood stove, and he knew what a beaver ought to do. Though he had no adult beaver to teach him, he realized that all sticks I gave him could be first nibbled at and then carefully stacked across the door of the kennel. Because no mud was available (even I have to draw a line somewhere), and because the sticks did not give enough privacy, he plundered the laundry basket and selected a large pink T-shirt.

This he wove around and over and in and out of the sticks — a dreadful tangle but an effective, dam-like barricade: a barricade that was supposed to be respected. Even if his ancestors did not have the foresight to obey the Creator, Swampy expected obedience from the world around him, especially from a raccoon kit named Snowman.

The first glimmerings of the strong territorial tendencies of beavers were soon evident. Snowman, in the nonchalant manner of all raccoons, scarcely noticing the stick-and-pink barricade, followed his inquisitive black nose into the kennel. From across the room, Swampy saw the invasion. He flew (beavers can clumsily, but effectively, almost fly) to the kennel. He flapped on Snowman's rear end. With teeth and hands he held on and hauled him out. Then he put a stranglehold on Snowman's head, trundled him halfway across the room, and, with an emphatic grunt, pushed him the rest of the way. With another grunt, end of discussion. Snowman had learned what a beaver barricade meant.

Beavers share willingly, generously, with their own families, and Swampy had selected his family. I was privileged to be most of it — a choice that was entirely his. He tolerated the skunk and the raccoon, he tolerated assorted cats, and he acknowledged the dogs. But he selected me as his friend. When I sat, he often pressed close to my ankles and sat too. Sometimes he put his hands on the cushion of the chair, and with the help of a thrust of his tail, heaved himself up beside me.

Sometimes, when he wanted attention, he would grab a small handful of the material of my slacks and tug. When I looked down, he would stretch up his arms. Always, he talked and talked; and of course, I responded. I am not certain about the literal content of those conversations, but to both of us they were special and important.

I must admit, I have always had a little bit of trouble believing authorities on any subject. When Swampy met his first biologist, I was told: "He must be a month old, his eyes are open." I protested, as I had

27

read in a biology book that beavers are born with their eyes open. The biologist snorted in contempt. "I raised a beaver once. When I got it, its eyes were closed." Perhaps it had some sort of cold, because the consensus, which I believe correct, is that beavers are born with eyes open.

Some biology books say that baby beavers swim immediately, others state that the introduction to water is delayed for some weeks after birth. I decided that Swampy would have to choose for himself. When I first came to the valley I wanted a lake, so I had a pond dug, complete with a small island. A creek, which ran through the meadow, would fill it and drain it too. I also dammed the outlet so that the water would deepen. At one end of the pond, the water was about two feet deep, at the other six or seven. Over the few years, cattails had grown, water lilies had appeared and some duckweed, minnows and frogs. Of course it had become a mecca for our raccoons and skunks. Now it would be a swimming hole for a beaver — I hoped.

Beavers, at least baby beavers, heel naturally, better than most trained dogs. And so, the little beaver at my heels, his small legs going as fast as possible earnestly trying to keep up with me, I took the path through the tall grass down to the pond. I hoped he would see the water and joyfully dive in. Instead, he stopped at the edge, stood up on his haunches and looked at me.

"That," I explained to him," is a pond. Water. Beavers like water."

He turned and started back up the trail. I picked him up and turned him once more to face the water.

"Beavers like water," I repeated. "Go in and swim."

Somewhere I had read (one biologist had observed) that beaver kits learn to swim by following their parents' example. Again, another biologist wrote, beaver kits are so eager to swim that the parents have to keep them out of the water until their oil glands are functioning properly. Well, I could but experiment. Kicking off my shoes, I waded into the pond. Mud oozed between my toes, slid over my feet, and flowed around my ankles.

"I wouldn't do this," I told the interested beaver, "for anyone but you." It was true.

As I waded through the sucking mud until I was waist deep in the water, he watched, considering. I waited. He waited. His nose twitched. Maybe, for a beaver, this was a huge decision. I was wondering how deep my legs would sink in the mud. How long would it take a beaver to make up its mind?

But he did. He ran in. He moved cleanly, swiftly, arrowing his way through the water as though he had known how to swim for a thousand years. Nose at the surface, hands tucked tightly against his chest, webbed back feet pushing strongly, he swam in larger-and-larger circles around me. Once, hind feet thrusting, he ventured a shallow dive.

A swimming beaver is graceful beyond imagining. The bulky body, so cumbersome on land, moves effortlessly and swiftly, diving, turning and suddenly still. Beavers are made for the water, on the surface and below it. Under the water, the velvet nostrils close, the ears seal themselves tight against the skull, and two skin flaps behind the orange front teeth close to prevent water from trickling down the throat. Oil, combed into the outer coat, keeps them dry. Swampy did not know any of these extraordinary facts; he just realized that he liked to swim.

Swampy wanted a swim every day, and the daily swim began to follow a pattern. First of all, he would swim without me. (For that I was very grateful. He could swim without contacting the bottom — I couldn't.) From beside the pond, I would watch as he paddled swiftly in larger-and-larger circles around and around the pond. Then, his first energy expended, he idled among the lily pads and the reeds and nosed along the edge of the island, venturing up the creek to play around the tangled roots of the alders. Where the creek flowed into the pond, a deep hole had developed. This, he seemed to feel, had to be somehow modified. He cut sticks, found sticks, and struggled with them to the hole. But when he tried to anchor them there, the current continually carried them away. Undeterred, patient, he replaced them. Eventually he would learn (and he did) to build a dam. To signal the end of his swim, Swampy glided to his launching place, pulled himself to land and, sitting on those bulky haunches, used his hands and mouth to groom. Then, suitably dry, he would plod purposefully up the path, through the gate and across the cut grass (never, at my house, a "lawn") to the porch. There, with some difficulty, he would hoist himself up the high step, cross the porch and begin to gnaw at the front door. I would let him in.

Perhaps it was this newly discovered joy of water that led the beaver to instigate a shift in the organization of my household.

Nighttime in my house can be full of rustlings. With concentration and long practice, I can burrow deep under my blankets and ignore the bumping of beasts and the thumping across the dark floors, under and over the furniture, on my bed. Morning, however, can present some surprises. One morning, about a month after the beaver's first swim, I was, before settling into my normal breakfast routine, saying hello to each creature. The dogs cheerfully wagged their way out to the dog run. Snowman contemplated his breakfast before he began to eat it enthusiastically and scatter it. The cats, home from a nighttime prowl, curled up and slept. Skunky, I presumed, was in his house under the vanity.

Beaver? His kennel was empty.

"Swampy!"

Snowman didn't pause — raccoons can seldom be distracted from their food. The cats didn't stir. The dogs were outside. I searched behind the sofa, behind the piano, under the stove, under the bed, in the laundry basket.

"Swampy!"

And finally, an answering grunt.

For two years, Skunky had slept, snuggled in his blanket, on the lowest shelf of the bathroom vanity. Now, at some time during the night, maybe because of the proximity to the bathtub, Swampy had decided to move in. And there he was, crowded in beside the skunk.

Beavers believe, I suppose, in the power of persistent pressure. Within two days, Skunky had abandoned his vanity for a more private residence under the chest of drawers in my bedroom. The bathroom belonged to the beaver.

Now Swampy had his own den, within the occasional sound of running water, and he had to furnish it. I quickly began to learn about the variety of unlikely objects (in addition to four-legged beasties) that can "go bump in the night." Scatter rugs slithered down the hall. Coffee mugs, left carelessly on the floor, bumped as the beaver tried to hold them high between his teeth. Plates scraped to a cache behind the toilet. Clothes made scarcely a whisper as they were pilfered from the laundry basket. Books, though, were noisier, as not only did they drag off shelves with a satisfying thump, but they could also be chewed, the pulp packed between sticks. In one night, Swampy digested large portions of the *Holy Bible*; the *I Hate to Cook* book and *The Complete Works of Alfred Lord Tennyson*. Brooms, dust mops, and canoe paddles clattered with dreadful delight, and since maneuvering them along the narrow hall and into the bathroom was difficult, they were often abandoned halfway down the hallway, creating an early-morning obstacle course.

Only once did Swampy attempt to furnish the bathroom. Late one evening, I was startled by a chair gliding quietly across the living room, Swampy straining mightily against a lower rung. However, the chair's leg snagged between a bookcase and the stair banister, although Swampy juggled it a while before he admitted defeat.

Though Swampy shared the bathroom when necessary, it was definitely his room. One rainy afternoon, when I had no inclination whatsoever to go wading in the pond, even to placate a restless beaver, I decided to compromise by bringing into the house a large armful of smallish aspen branches. If he had been a human child given bowls full of candy and toys, he couldn't have been more delighted. Mumbling happily, he sorted through the pile, nose and hands busily investigating every single branch. What mental process was at work I cannot guess, however some branches were selected to be carried away first, angled up the hallway and through the bathroom door. All afternoon he worked, grunting, pulling, pushing, rearranging. I continued my work, uninterrupted. Whose work was more important? I don't remember exactly what I was doing, but he certainly accomplished a work of art!

By evening, I realized that silence had descended on the household. Swampy was asleep, snoring softly in the vanity. The aspen dam he had built extended the full length of the bathtub and completely surrounded the toilet. He had dammed off all the running water. His vanity lodge was safe and dry.

Although the beaver is Canada's national symbol, and crouches docilely on our nickel where we are quite familiar with him, few people have ever been close to an actual, live beaver. Over the years, the beavers and I have visited many, many schools and clubs. But the first public appearance was at Killbear Provincial Park, north of Parry Sound. We had been invited to speak to a large group of campers gathered in the outdoor amphitheatre. That is, I had been invited to speak. Swampy went with me. He was supposed to illustrate the work we do. He had other ideas.

From the moment I had taken him out of the car, he had quietly allowed the children who crowded him to admire his orange teeth, his leathery tail, and his gleaming brown fur. At the appropriate time, with Swampy still in my arms, I stepped to the microphone. I was to talk about our work with all the creatures at the Sanctuary and, of course, beavers. For several moments, Swampy, along with the campers, listened quietly. Then apparently he decided he was more of an authority than I was. He grunted into the microphone, paused, and then squealed into it. The squeal was amplified all around the theatre. He listened, then squeaked again, loving the laughter and applause greeting his every declaration. His lecture was a huge success.

Do animals remember? Two weeks later when we again stood in front of a microphone, he didn't wait for me to begin. He launched immediately into his own speech, this time accompanied by much shaking of the head and fist waving — either an evangelist or a politician! Maybe being the symbol of Canada was going to his head. Or maybe he agreed with the rest of us at the Sanctuary that the education of children is of vital importance. For the more informed and experienced a person becomes with wild creatures, the greater an appreciation they develop for them — an appreciation that will lead, hopefully, to caring. Our beavers are frequent educators, and we try to be absolutely accurate, no matter what the situation. After all, who could be more accurate than the beavers themselves?

The general store in Rosseau was small, historic, and in the tourist season, very crowded. There one summer I met a couple, young, with two extremely polite children. They were visiting the Rosseau area from Europe.

"We are going home next week," the mother explained in careful English. "We would like to have seen your national symbol."

Of course I invited them to come to the Sanctuary and meet our own special symbol. And fortunately, I arrived at the house about ten minutes ahead of them. The beaver who came thumping out of the bathroom to meet me was no longer the glossy brown of the Canadian symbol. He had discovered my paint box.

"Swampy," I scolded sternly, "we cannot let those children think that the symbol of Canada is cadmium yellow, medium."

Just because beavers like water does not mean they like to be scrubbed. He struggled mightily. I won. When the children arrived, Swampy was wet, but brown. The only cadmium yellow, medium that remained was the wandering highway line his tail had dragged all over the house.

AND THEN THERE WERE TWO

If a human being truly wants a luxurious, well-appointed bathroom, then that human being should have a luxurious, well-appointed bathroom; however, under certain situations, such a bathroom is not possible — a choice must be made. A perfect bathroom? Or a beaver?

Recently, reminiscing about those early days, a friend said, uncritically, "Ah yes, I remember going into your bathroom and having to step over laundry, long sticks and short sticks and assorted kitchen utensils." Politely, he did not mention the mud. Beavers love mud.

Obviously, and for different reasons, both Swampy and I realized that he needed a small outdoor pond. I could not leave a small beaver unsupervised in our large pond — he might wander too far away or a passing fisher or coyote might, quite naturally, consider him a fine meal. And I would not carry into the house sufficient mud to content a beaver.

But mud was a necessity.

A bathtub is no substitute for a pond; a real pond with flowing water, green growing things and lots of mud — especially mud. For every beaver should have as much mud as possible.

Outside the house, in the valley, mud was readily available. A constantly running ribbon of water dribbled out of a spring under the tall pines on the side of the east hill. Not large enough to show itself through the grass, the water wandered in a leisurely way down towards the house. I decided that a pond built just across the laneway from the door would be suitable and convenient for both of us, and not hard to dig.

A fence would have to surround the pond, high enough that wandering coyotes would not scale it and deep enough underground that a beaver (skilled tunnellers that they are) would not go under. So I sat down and began to add up the costs. The digging I could do myself. The water would collect naturally. But fencing, even for a ten-by-twenty-foot enclosure, was expensive. And beavers would be able to cut down wooden posts, so steel was needed. Assorted types of hardware would be necessary to hold it together. I also had to add in labor costs, realizing that I couldn't build it by myself. When everything I could imagine was included, the total cost was well beyond my limited budget. What price mud?

However, at this point Swampy plodded directly into the heart of a television host from CKCO, Kitchener. Betty Thompson, host of a morning television program called *Tempo*, visited the Sanctuary to do a short news item on the rehabilitation of the wild creatures. First she met Bucky. Bucky was a small, spotted fawn who had had an unfortunate encounter with some hunting dogs. Despite losing a hind leg he managed very well, frisking about his enclosure and suckling on his bottle as hungrily as a normal fawn. He was filmed for the show. Betty liked him very much. Then she met a few frisky squirrels ready for release, tails flicking impatiently. They were filmed. She met small, round raccoon kits, eyes full of intelligence and mischief. She met and filmed a fox kit and a skunk. But she fell in love with the beaver.

That October, I received a phone call from CKCO. Betty had realized that a beaver should never be confined to a mud-free bathtub. Could I bring Swampy down to the studio in Kitchener?

"Yes." I was hesitant. "Why?"

"We're going to have a telethon. We're going to raise enough money to build the enclosure."

Betty Thompson really, really cared. And Swampy would have mud.

A few weeks later, long before dawn, my niece Janet (visiting from Nova Scotia), Swampy and I climbed into the car and began the four-hour drive to Kitchener. We had to be there by nine o'clock. To keep me awake, Janet chatted cheerfully. Swampy slept. I doubt that he knew he was in a car being driven to star in his very own television special. Now, I admit that I do not like driving, and my knowledge of highways is hazy, so Janet, map on knee, was the navigator. We drove south through mile after mile of darkness. Finally, Janet slept.

South of Barrie, the sun rose. Briefly, light filtered across the countryside. Then the rain began, a driving rain indicating we just might not arrive at the studio on time — that Swampy's public career might not be about to begin. Water washed across the highways; the windshield wipers were almost ineffective. Familiar landmarks and signs were obliterated. I had to drive slowly. I couldn't read the map. I poked Janet. She woke up. Swampy slept on.

However, a mere fifteen minutes before the telethon was to begin, we did arrive. The program director was pacing anxiously between three raised chairs sitting empty on a dais and the entrance from which, carrying the cage between us, Janet and I, wet and triumphant, finally erupted. Quickly, I was ushered to one of the chairs, Swampy's cage at my feet. Swampy was to stay in his cage.

I protested. "He can't do his special in a cage!" To which the director answered shortly, "And he can't mess on our new carpet!"

Having more faith in a beaver's bladder than he did, I answered: "I'll keep him on my knee." So I settled Swampy on my lap. He slept on.

The little red light flashed. With great animation, Betty began talking towards the appropriate camera. She explained to the great Canadian viewing public how this beaver, the symbol of Canada, had been orphaned, and, living in captivity all his life, needed a pond. She did not mention mud. She talked about the injured fawn, about the squirrels and about the raccoons; mostly she talked about Swampy. The camera focused on him. He slept on.

Then the phones began to ring. I was amazed — and touched — that so many people would care enough for an orphaned baby beaver that they would donate money to help him. I also felt that Swampy should show some appreciation, so I shifted him on my knee (certainly, although nature dictates that beavers should doze through the day, not every beaver has his very own show). I shook him gently. He slept on. But even in his sleep he was charming.

People phoned in their pledges; the phones kept ringing. I began to realize that Swampy would have his pond, and his mud. The director was happy. Betty was happy. I was happy. And Swampy . . . I jiggled him on my knee and pinched his fat belly just a little. He grunted. He pushed my hand away. And slept on.

That month the new pen was built, a beautiful pen with running water and a pond, a lodge (human-made at first) and mud. The enclosure was just across the laneway from the house. When he wanted to visit, Swampy would sit at his gate and stare at my door. I would go to him and open the gate, and he would trundle after me up the steps and into the house. And I made the discovery that the addition of a pond did not mean that I would once again have a beaver-free house. It simply meant that Swampy had a larger choice of living space.

He did prefer the pond to the bathtub, which I reclaimed for myself — temporarily. Temporarily, I had a beautiful, clean bathroom. I began to make plans. I might have the door, with its magnificent teeth marks and beaver arch, replaced with a new, entire door. I could put new linoleum on the floor and know it would not be gnawed by a bored beaver. The black scar marks in the enamel bathtub I would have to live with, a memento of the strength of the beaver's teeth. But overall, at last, warm bath mats, gleaming cleanliness. . . .

I had arrived at the point of discussing the renovation of the bathroom with a friendly carpenter. Then the phone rang.

I answered, of course. This was the month of June, the usual busy month when wild babies are born and so often orphaned, our busiest month for squirrels and raccoons, skunks and foxes.

A cottager from Lake Muskoka was calling. "We have found a baby beaver," she said, "and we don't know what to do with it. It has been swimming around our island for a day and a half crying. We finally couldn't stand it anymore, so we called it and it came and we have it."

A baby beaver. A little, round, brown, baby beaver.

"Well," I replied, trying to sound casual instead of covetous, afraid they would want it for a pet. "Beavers are difficult to raise. And you have to keep it always — a hand-raised beaver does not adapt to the wild. And it will need goat's milk, and of course a pond." (I still believed the biology books.)

I really didn't need to sound so discouraging. The lady did not want to keep the kit. However, she listened politely, and with no trace of exasperation asked, "Would you like it? Will you take it?"

"Yes." Never a thought for a nice, clean bathroom, not a single thought, only thoughts about a little, round, brown beaver kit, fat and squeaky.

The wait between the phone call and the arrival of the car bringing the people and the kit up the laneway was not long, and the kit, so small I could hold it in one hand, nestled in my arms. Another beaver — another little beaver. I held it down to the enclosure gate so that Swampy, drawn in by the car's arrival, could see it. He looked, grunted, and trundled back to the water, completely uninterested.

The little beaver had not been taken away from its parents; the people who brought him truly cared about wild things and knew that the best possible choice for the kit would have been for it to be raised by its own parents. Sometime during the afternoon they had heard it swimming around and around their island and crying. They did not interfere. They reasoned that, after sunset, the mother beaver would respond to the cries of distress. But she did not come. Likely, something had happened to her and she could not. Beavers care intensely for their families; she would not have carelessly abandoned her kit. On into the night, the kit swam and cried. At four in the morning, the people went out and answered the crying. The little beaver came to them. They picked it out of the water, wrapped it in a warm sweater and cuddled it close. Content, it slept.

Now, suckling goat's milk from a warm bottle, "Beaver" established himself firmly in my household and my heart. It began with Swampy, and now, beyond any doubt, beavers became the greatest delight of my life.

Beavers! The beaver most familiar to most of us is the animal whose placid profile we see on our Canadian nickel. We see the same flat creature pasted on top of the coat of arms. If we believed these portraits, the common expression "busy as a beaver" would be completely irrelevant. Perhaps the skipping beaver advertising the Beaver Lumber Company is more accurate, though one suspects that particular symbolic beaver is more irresponsible than a real beaver.

Rarely, from the lofty heights from which we humans observe creatures, do we see beyond the patterns of their lives to the joy that they often know. That animals can know joy may not be more than mere speculation, of course, but it's consistent with my experience with animals. Maybe (speculation again) that is the reason God did not confine creation only to humans. God wanted creation to be joyous. God made ravens to slide, circle and float with wide-spread wings on the high air currents. God made otters to slip and slide down muddy banks and tumble in the water. God made turtles to bask luxuriously in the hot sunshine. Taking walks with raccoons, I have tried to see the world through their eyes — bouncing, happy creatures who scuttle beneath the shady undergrowth and then scamper up to the sun-speckled tree tops. I have watched the quiver of excitement of skunks moving among mossy stones. And I have swum in the pond with beavers and seen them swirl and dive and stretch their sleek bodies in the pure ecstasy of the moment.

These two beavers would introduce me to puzzles and joys; the reality of beaver life. Though in my role of caregiver I would learn through good guesses and sad mistakes much about beavers, the greatest privilege would be to allow them to teach me — slowly, emphatically, patiently, willingly. They would share their lives with me.

QUIBBLE

Swampy and Little Beaver (he never acquired any other name except Beaver, perhaps because he was the quintessential beaver) helped me begin to understand that beavers are far more individual and intelligent than biology books or national symbols ever indicated. Over the years they lived with me, I learned that they were not pets. They became, in a very real sense, my friends.

In the wild, because of the intensity of trapping, predators, and disease, the average lifespan of a beaver is between four and five years. Swampy and Little Beaver lived that and then they died, and for a while I felt a deep loneliness. And then came Quibble!

Not far outside Orillia, at the back of a farm, a small stream winds through a woodlot and a small meadow. Quietly one night, a pair of beavers moved up the stream looking for somewhere to call home. They found a place. They cut scrub aspen and alders. They dug and carried mud. They built a dam. A pond formed. They built a lodge, warm inside and dry. After a long winter, they had a family. The surrounding trees and meadows flourished. Wildlife — deer and raccoons, ducks, fish and frogs — all were glad to have such a supply of water. Only the farmer didn't like it. He took a few sticks of dynamite and tossed them into the lodge.

When the dynamite blew, spewing sticks and mud high into the air, the beavers were killed. All except one very small beaver kit. He was blown out into the meadow, where he landed, somehow unhurt, totally bewildered and utterly alone. Two little girls, playing in the meadow, found him and recognized a small, completely captivating little being in desperate need of help. They picked him up. He snuggled trustingly in their arms. They took him home.

Kind children tend to have kind parents — and wise. They knew that one little beaver, an orphaned wild creature needing warmth and food and love, would grow into a great big beaver needing the wilderness. A tiny beaver might weigh one pound; an adult beaver might weigh sixty. So the little girls were allowed to keep their beaver for a couple of weeks. They bottle fed him, gave him apples and bananas, and let him swim in shallow water in the bathtub. In short, they did the very best they could, and the little beaver lived.

However, he was beginning to grow, so arrangements were made to bring him to the Sanctuary. Kathy and Sylvia, the little girls, were well prepared for and accepting of the surrendering of their kit. With shining eyes, they told me how exciting it had been to help a beaver kit.

"He swam in the bathtub. He splashed his tail!"

"He likes apples . . . and bananas."

"He talks! He talks a lot!"

Though they had been taught that he must be free to grow up and be a real beaver, they had loved him dearly.

I could not name a third beaver simply "Beaver." So I was faced with a situation I still find difficult — selecting a name. The poet T. S. Eliot wrote an entire poem about the naming of cats. He wrote:

The naming of cats is a difficult matter.
It isn't just one of your holiday games.
You may think at first that I'm mad as a hatter
When I tell you a cat must have three different names.

Three! At the beginning, for some obscure reason even I don't remember, each Sanctuary beaver had to have a name beginning with the letter Q. We had Quimby and Quimber, Quinty, Quetico and Qualicum. Quaker had arrived at the Sanctuary because of an injury and was somewhat older. If we approached him, deeply resenting humans and captivity he would slap his tail furiously on the water of his wading pond. Now, being in close proximity to an angry adult beaver slapping its tail, even in a wading pond, can result in a drenching equivalent to being caught in a sudden and violent thunderstorm. Thus he earned the name Earthquake, or Quaker.

41

The kit that Kathy and Sylvia brought to the Sanctuary became Quibble. I can't quite explain the choice, as he was not really argumentative and Quibble really did not reflect his personality. But if the meaning of the word is separated from the sound, the sound itself is rather fun — a tripping sound, like small drops of water bouncing down a waterfall. The word dribble might be more appropriate, but one can't name a beaver Dribble. Thus he became Quibble.

Kathy and Sylvia had been very good to the orphaned beaver, and beavers form strong family affections. Ideally, "family" implies warmth, support, understanding and love, and although human families do not necessarily have all these attributes, animal families often rate very highly. Wolves are well known for the strength of their family relationships. The wolf family, alpha and beta wolves and their pups, will be cared for by aunts, uncles and older siblings. The beaver family is very much the same. So Quibble was attached to the girls, and being parted from them could have been a bit traumatic, except that another little beaver, Quimby, was living at the Sanctuary. Quibble's memory of his own beaver family was still strong, and he and Quimby became friends. However, Quibble did not forget the children.

Unfortunately, Quimby had been the victim of the kind of people who come to Muskoka for a summer wilderness experience but bring with them city values. Forgetting that the beavers have lived here for centuries, keeping our lakes full and our forests green, the humans arrive and discover a beaver wanting to use part of their boathouse for a lodge (the beaver doesn't realize that cool, dark places are not built especially for him). The humans panic, and, refusing to enjoy or learn from the beaver or even to share with it, they demand that it be removed or shot.

Quimby's family had found an empty, dark, sheltered boathouse, had lived quietly until the city invasion, and then had been turned out quickly. I don't think that the beavers deliberately forgot the one, very tiny kit, I believe the assault on the lodge was too chaotic and quick

Quibble makes himself a home.

and thorough. Had they been allowed, the parents would have returned and taken the kit with them.

Instead, the kit had been kidnapped, brought miles to the Sanctuary and thrust at us. He was so tiny! We made a small enclosure in the house for him and gave him a small pan of water. We gave him a baby bottle of goat's milk five times a day. But he was very, very young. He needed his mother's milk and he needed his family. No human can fill these needs, especially not for a newborn beaver kit.

When Quibble came, though, he was larger than Quimby, and I hoped the companionship of another beaver would cure the loneliness of the very little kit. For a while I thought it had. The beavers slept, curled close together. As they munched their apples and yams, cherries and peaches, they chatted with each other. They wrestled. And for a while, I hoped. But Quimby stopped eating, grew gradually weaker and died.

Quibble mourned, almost angrily. He murmured. He paced. His short life had been full of loss. He crawled on to my lap, and had he been human, I would have said the soft, soft whimpering was really weeping. We walked outside. We swam in the large pond. We became good friends. But I was not a beaver.

The Sanctuary still had the enclosure that had been built for Swampy: pond, underground fencing, lots of mud and enough branches supplied to keep a beaver happy. Quibble could sleep in a small, dark, hay-filled kennel covered with sticks. (I could not build a real lodge. That is strictly beaver ability.) During the day, as long as I stopped by and spent some time with him, he was quite content. But he had no intention of spending the night alone. Towards the end of each afternoon, he would sit on his fat haunches by the gate, grasp the wire in his hands and rattle it. He wanted in the house! When I opened the gate, he would trundle purposefully across the lane, up the steps, across the porch (I would have the door open) into the house and the kitchen. Food.

He made nests for himself inside the house, often changing location as though searching for the proper place. The material was much the same as Swampy had selected: wood from the wood bin, laundry, bowls from my shelves, brooms, shoes, books — anything portable. He moved it all from place to place. Under the couch, under the table, up against a tipped-over chair, and in the bathroom. The bathroom! Gradually, as it had for Swampy, the bathroom became a favorite place, with its warmth and water! But no mud. Mud, I was still firmly insistent, was outside only.

Next to his outside enclosure, sharing the south fence, was a second enclosure where a young silver fox named Jack Frost lived. When the little beaver was first put into the enclosure, Jack had been very curious. And though Quibble had taken a while longer to realize that his neighbor was unusual, his curiosity finally overcame his caution. I found them meditating on each other, almost nose to nose, through the fence. I was quite certain the beaver would not damage the fox, but I was not certain the fox would feel quite so benign about the beaver. Imagining Quibble's small hands reaching tentatively through the fence and being badly bitten, I decided to line the lower part of the fence with small-gauge chicken wire.

Beavers begin working when they are quite young, imitating their parents and older siblings, "helping." The fence-reinforcing job wasn't difficult. As I worked, Jack was watching me carefully, maybe critically, his head cocked to one side, his ears forward. Jack was a refugee from a fur farm. Instead of becoming a fur coat, he was destined to learn about the fields and forests that surrounded us, and to live free. Now, he could feel the warm sun and the soft wind. He could hear the birds high above us. As I worked, cutting and twisting wire, I chatted to the fox and to Quibble and enjoyed the morning quiet.

Then, suddenly, I heard the gurgle of water behind me. I stopped working and turned. A stout little beaver, arms full of dripping mud, was moving earnestly up the bank. He brought the mud to the fence and began plugging the chicken wire with it, filling the holes, seriously and industriously. Even when I considered the fence finished, Quib still worked hard. He reinforced the entire length with mud and sticks, totally ignoring the puzzled Jack Frost.

Quibble had a lot of work to do in his life, not only real beaver work, but human work, mostly educating people. Educating children is a part of any live-in beaver's responsibilities at the Sanctuary; the more close, personal contact a child has with a living animal, the more likely the child is to respect and to begin to understand it. The Sanctuary also does a great deal of work in the schools, and both Swampy and Beaver had enjoyed these contacts. But Quibble did not seem to enjoy the educational responsibilities he had inherited. The only real explanation I can find may subject me to much criticism for being sexist, but I do plead that this is a biological, not a sexist explanation.

Beavers have no external sex organs, so short of a great deal of internal poking and probing (difficult with an unwilling beaver), or an equally uncomfortable X-ray, the matter of gender is merely a guess. Now here's where I court trouble! Female beavers are usually quite amiable. The males are more aggressive and territorial. On this flimsy evidence, I wondered, if Swampy and Beaver had, perhaps, been female and Quibble male.

That first autumn when I took him to schools, which I did often, he was merely tolerant. He allowed himself to be viewed, discussed and appreciated — but certainly not touched. When I walked around a circle of children sitting on the floor, he would follow closely at my heels — once only. Knowing he did not like them to touch him, I would say to the children, "Just look." He totally ignored everything but my heels.

The last week of school before the Christmas holiday began, and Quibble and I were invited to a school in Orillia. I carried him, in a small kennel, into the gymnasium, where seventy-six children sat in a large circle, waiting for us. I sat in the circle, Quib on my knee, and talked about beavers. I showed the children his teeth, his hands and feet and, of course, his tail. I told them about the many ways beavers are specially equipped for life in the water: the special film to cover their eyes, the skin flap inside their mouths, the special oil for their fur, and the ability to seal their ears closed. All of this Quibble endured patiently.

As I had done in a dozen other schools, knowing he would completely and patiently ignore his surroundings, I put him on the floor and started around the circle so the children could see him. His eyes steadfastly on my heels, we moved slowly and steadily. I heard the flip-flop of his feet. Heard it. And then I didn't. I turned. The heeling beaver, having ignored forty or fifty children, placidly avoiding any reaching hand, deaf to the delighted squeals, had stopped. He stopped, sat up on his haunches, peered short-sightedly, grunted, then crawled up on the lap of one of the children. He had found Kathy. After all the schools he had visited, all the children he had endured and ignored, out of the seventy-six children who sat in that circle, he had found, and remembered, Kathy, part of his first human family!

Recently, a Native friend of mine was sitting in my living room. We had been discussing a small bear who had just been brought, starving and sick, to the Sanctuary. Conversation waned a little, and my friend looked around the room. A small smile creased the corners of his eyes. Finally he said: "They all get along, don't they?" The three dogs slept, one back-to-back with a cat. Another cat slept among the houseplants around a large bird cage, where an injured dove was also sleeping within two inches of the cats. "That's the way it was in the beginning," he said.

I expect he was right.

Animals can get along. Once, along with the dogs and cats, a raccoon kit and a young groundhog roamed my house and slept together in a kennel by the woodstove. The only objection the groundhog had was that the raccoon refused to use the litter box. One of my Labs, Abby, was great friends with a duck named Archie — they roamed the fields together. Another winter Moon, the raccoon, slept warmly in the house with a skunk, Dugan. After Moon returned to the wild, Dugan made good friends with a pup, Duncan. Quibble adjusted equally well into my turbulent household, except there was one limit. His apple.

Some years ago a friend, Doris, was roaming flea markets in Toronto and found a fantastic Fisher Price apple. It had a smile on its face and a lovely chime inside. Knowing that this was a perfect raccoon toy, she sent it up to the Sanctuary. Undoubtedly, because it was from a flea market, it had endured many children's playing hours. Now it became the favorite plaything of litter after litter of raccoons. Then it became the toy of Quibble, and Quibble loved his roly-poly apple. When he pushed it around with his nose, the apple chimed. He rocked it, he wrestled with it — it was a wonderful, wonderful toy. He stored it under the desk and nobody dared to touch it. When I thought it was time for Quibble to put away childish things, I took his apple and stored it.

A year later, a very small, orphaned bear cub joined our household. He decimated almost every toy I gave him. Teddy bears lasted only a day or so. Tennis balls grew boring. At last, I remembered the chiming, roly-poly apple. The cub played with it. He slept with it. Finally he grew big enough that he could go to an outdoor enclosure, and the apple went back into storage.

One day, Quibble seemed lethargic, perhaps bored. I thought perhaps he might like to play with the apple. I brought it out. He sniffed it. He chased it all over the house. Then he hid it under the couch, stuffed a rug in to make sure it stayed there, and, with a great huff of displeasure, he left it.

Later that year, I was given a young cougar, Teka. Teka had been bought at an auction sale, taken home as a cute kitten and, naturally, proceeded to grow into a very big cat. For a year, she was confined to a concrete-floored garage. From there, she was rescued by the local police and sent to us. This animal I did not bring into the house! Until I found a good country place for her to live (declawed, she could not go free), she had her fairly large outdoor enclosure. I did not want her to be bored. She needed toys. I remembered the apple. The cougar's great, soft, declawed paws batted the apple around, and she purred in response to its charming chime.

However, sharing had its limits. After the cougar had left us, I brought the apple back into the house and casually left it on a chair. Quibby, wandering, found it and smelled cougar. That was enough. He knocked the apple down the cellar stairs and it went bounce-chime, bounce-chime, all the way down. Then I heard it being pushed and chimed all over the basement. I heard great huffing and puffing. The huffing and puffing went on for a long time. I went away for an hour, and when I returned I heard a fainter chime and fewer huffs and puffs. By nightfall, all was silent. The next day I went down to the basement to investigate, and found one beaver fast asleep, bits of red all over the place. The Fisher Price apple had been totally destroyed. All that was left was the core and the little wee chimes, which now let out a pitiful tiny, mewing sound. No beaver should ever be asked to share with a cougar.

QUETICO

Way back at the turn of the century, Bear Cave Road was the track for logging wagons hauling the trunks of giant spruce and pine out to the lumber mills on the Rosseau River. It was a rough track over big granite rocks, through deep ponds and puddles, and around, down and up through a quiet wilderness. After a while, miles out the road, a log house was built, meadows were cleared, and a farm came into being. The log house was beside a clean, fast-flowing stream — a stream large enough that the loggers had to build a small bridge to cross it.

The years passed. The great trees disappeared. For a while, the farm prospered. But then, since it was a distance by horse and wagon to the general store in Rosseau and the trees began to encroach as the forest renewed itself, it was abandoned. The beavers built a series of dams, and the stream became a small, shallow lake with cattails, pickerel weed and water lilies. The only humans who disturbed the peace were the trappers, for foxes, raccoons, mink and beaver pelts. Hunters came, too, seeking deer, moose and bears. Wolves moved silently through the shadows.

Time passed. The human population, first in search of free land and good farms (the farms were not very prosperous!), and then, still later, in search of summer fun, pressed north into Muskoka. Bear Cave Road was discovered as a nice place for a slow, very careful evening drive — one might see almost any kind of wildlife. A couple of hunt camps were built, and the rutted road was used more often, except in the winter.

Finally, the road was a shortcut for school buses. Winter use became necessity. One could travel the length of the road and never encounter any wildlife. Still, two or three cars a day indicated heavy traffic. The bridge was improved. The little lake still bloomed with the purple of pickerel weed and water iris, with yellow bull lilies and white water lilies. But the beaver lodges were empty.

A good friend became aware of the necessity for remote release areas for the animals that had been cared for at the Sanctuary. She bought four hundred and twenty-five acres out on Bear Cave Road — acreage backing on miles of crown land, acreage that included the little lake and the empty beaver lodges.

"The land is for the animals," she stipulated. "Let them go free there." So now out the pioneer road is a large area, safe for wildlife, where the great trees are growing again. Raccoons, skunks and foxes roam freely, and — once more, in the lake — beaver. Especially one very exceptional beaver: Quetico!

Because we have details of his life from the time he was orphaned, and also his life after he was given his freedom, I find Quetico a beaver of very special interest.

Quetico was born in a lodge out among the reeds in a wetland on the outskirts of Ottawa. There, a mother beaver gave birth to two tiny, furry brown kits, their small black eyes open and alert. All around the lodge, the wetland was green with spring. Water lily plants were thrusting upward through the water. Frogs were singing. And, in the warm darkness of the lodge, the kits suckled contentedly.

In the city itself, a planner studied a map. His only concern was making life more convenient for humans. After a while he drew a satisfied breath and, with a sharpened pencil, tapped a single spot. "Here," he said. "The road will go through here."

Someone may have protested. "We'll have to drain a swamp. And the beaver . . . ."

"Fill it in," he probably ordered. "And get rid of the beaver."

The planners hired a trapper. Since beaver pelts are worthless in the spring, he did not take his traps. He took his gun. Standing quiet and still on the dam, he waited. When the mother beaver left the lodge and surfaced to feed, he shot her.

In the warm darkness of the lodge, the two kits whimpered with hunger. A day and a night and another day passed before the kits swam, timidly, down the tunnel of their lodge and out into the soft spring air. They called and called until at last, when their mother did not come, they huddled together on the shore of the wetland, lonely, hungry, and doomed.

However, the Ottawa-Carleton Wildlife Centre is staffed with people who care. They heard about the proposed road, and about the shooting of the mother beaver, and they knew that spring is the time when the kits are born.

One of the volunteers went down to the wetland. Because she arrived just ahead of the rumbling bulldozers, she was able to hear the hungry whimpering of the kits. They were not afraid of her — wild things have to learn fear. She picked them up, wrapped them in warm blankets and put them into a dark kennel. Then she took them to the Rehabilitation Centre. There, they were fed and kept warm. They had a small pool. They began to grow.

The Rehabilitation Centre was full of spring babies: squirrels and raccoons, woodchucks, foxes, deer and two little beavers. Usually, these animals are given their freedom at about the time they would, living naturally, have left their own families. For beaver, that time is at least two years — a long time to care for wild animals in an urban facility.

So, on the exceedingly strict understanding that, as soon as the kits were sufficiently mature they would be set free, they were lent to an education center, where a large pond was available to them. At the center people could learn about the sun, the moon and the stars, the seas, the deserts and the forests, and also beavers.

No matter how good the intention, being on constant public display is difficult for any wild-born creature. Beavers — intelligent, independent, born for the stillness of wetland and woodland — are no exception. And the kit we would come to know as Quetico for some reason especially disliked people. Though he could not have known that his own home had become a roadway, he probably realized that some violence had separated him from his mother, and he was a very angry animal.

He bit human hands offering food. He lunged at his sister, a most unnatural act since beavers are generally gentle with their siblings. He drummed with his tail. He splashed at the spectators. Back and forth he swam, back and forth, thrashing at the confines of his enclosure. Still, no matter how angry he was, he was still only a kit. Two years on display? Two years in a rock pool? Quetico grew more and more angry.

His keepers recognized his frustration — the high level of his stress. So the phone call came to the Sanctuary. "We have a beaver kit who is giving real problems," the keeper began. "Could we bring him to you?"

"Yes!" Of course. The enclosure that had been Quibble's had been empty long enough. Quite long enough! Quetico would have running water and lots of aspen, mud and privacy.

When we put Quetico into the enclosure, he seemed to inspect it carefully. He found the wire fence too high, too deep to tunnel under, and too tough to tear apart. But he had mud. The mud was the glory of his new enclosure. With mud, and the branches very bountifully supplied, he could work like a beaver. Though he had never been taught by parent beavers, he knew what he wanted to do and how to do it. Sensing the directions of the flow of the water, he cut and transported sticks. He carried and packed mud. The sticks he carried behind his big, orange teeth, chiselling, tugging, and towing them. The mud he cradled in great globs in his arms, pressed against his chest.

As the dam grew higher, he walked up it on his hind feet, carrying mud, packing mud. As the dam gained height, the water became deeper. Finally, he was satisfied.

Quetico goes free.

Still, he did not rest. Winter was coming. He needed a good lodge. In one corner of the enclosure was a wire cage roofed with plywood, the top and sides shielded with evergreen branches. Other beavers had found this at least acceptable housing. Not Quetico! Again, mud. From the bottom of his pond he dredged more mud. He carried armload after armload up to the cage. He plastered the walls, inside and out. He plastered the roof, inside and out. When he finally finished, he had a dark, warm lodge.

I said, "Winter is coming. He will have to go into the barn." But incredibly fast, incredibly good at disappearing even in the small enclosure, he seemed to say, "Leave me alone. I am a beaver. I can survive here and I will!"

Through the floor of his lodge, he dug a tunnel out to beneath the surface of the water. When the temperature dropped and the water froze over, he swam beneath it, a slim, moving shadow. When he

53

wanted aspen, he broke the ice and pulled it in. We dropped apples and yams through the ventilation hole he had known to make in the top of his lodge.

I could not help realizing that, even without parents to teach him, the orphaned kit had known exactly what to do. He had not read the research insisting that he would not, alone, understand.

After the cold had frozen the water surface, the snow began to fall silently out of low, gray skies. The temperature dropped down and down into deep winter. I worried. Quetico did not. Even when the temperature dropped to minus twenty-two degrees Fahrenheit (-30C), and only deep silence emerged from the lodge, the food offerings I dropped into the vent seemed to disappear. January and February were long, long months.

March! The sun began to grow warmer. Though the snow was still deep, if I listened carefully I could hear, beneath the ice, the sound of running water. About the middle of the month, on a day when one could imagine a faint warmth in the sunlight, from a tunnel of snow, Quetico emerged. He was fat, sleek, glistening — and still angry. By April, the snow had gone and green things were growing, and Quetico, now a very healthy two-year-old, was demanding his freedom. He hurried frantically around and around the perimeters of his enclosure. Release time had come.

Finding a safe release site for beavers is difficult. The chosen area should not be home to any other beaver family. Being territorial, it is likely the resident beaver will drive an interloper away. Second, the food supply must be ample, making it easier for inexperienced and single beavers to maintain themselves. And since humans are the most dangerous of beaver predators, the release site has to be relatively remote from human habitation. Above all, there mustn't be any traplines anywhere. Such a place is almost impossible to find — but not quite.

Bear Cave Road, with its quiet little lake, empty beaver lodge, and safety! The property out there was as safe as any place close to human population can be, but we had had to fight for that safety.

After the property had become part of the Sanctuary, I admit I enjoyed that first morning of the duck-hunting season. I knew the duck hunters would be out at dawn. In previous years I had seen them, rifles ready, lining the bridge across the stream. This time I was up before dawn and, as the light grew in the east, my canoe, my dog and I were sitting some fifty feet offshore, waiting. The hunters came.

"We've been hunting here for years!" they yelled. Too bad.

"You'd better get out of the way!" No!

"This is no way to stay on good terms with your neighbors!" Alas.

Now the wetland has finally become a quiet place. Way out, at the edge of the far shore sat an old, abandoned beaver lodge. To me, the empty lodge seemed to need a beaver. And Quetico definitely needed a lodge.

Even in the small enclosure, catching Quetico was a challenge. He had to be herded away from his tunnel and his lodge and, hopefully, scooped out in a very strong net.

Beavers have incredible strength. They propel themselves with their great, webbed back feet and broad tail and, being rodents, can leap to attack. Their teeth, used only as a last defence, are as sharp as knives. So we knew capturing Quetico would not be easy, and it was not. However, we managed to drive him up on land and scooped with the net until he was pushed into a kennel. He trembled with fury.

Quetico could not know that the terrifying confusion — the kennel, the car, the long, rough road, and the transfer to the canoe — was the necessary prelude to his freedom. At least the canoe ride was quiet. Perhaps he sensed the trees (tall spruce, pine and aspen, reflected in the still water), the lily pads, and the reeds. Maybe he began to understand the sound of the dipping paddles. Perhaps he felt the slight jolt as the canoe nosed into the far shore.

And so we lifted the kennel to the forest floor, opened it and stood back. For a long, long moment, Quetico did not move. He raised himself a little, nostrils dilated, hands clenched. Then, slowly, cautiously, he took his first step — no cage door, no fence.

Suddenly he was out! He stopped. He stood tall. He looked. Then he was down on all fours, leaping to the water's edge. Smoothly, soundlessly he slid in, heading out into the open water. Then he turned back to the shore and clambered in among the reeds and out to the water again.

We collected the empty kennel, put it into the canoe and paddled away, leaving him alone. Free.

The gift of freedom is ours to give. But when we release, always we feel some apprehension. We could no longer guarantee Quetico's food supply, his shelter, or his safety. The wetland and the surrounding woods could be full of dangers. Was he prepared? Did he know what to do? Would he survive? As we paddled away, we wished him well. And we prayed a little.

That first night I kept thinking about him — the sunset, the darkness coming, the stars, the slow-rising moon, night birds, frogs, wolves calling deep in the woods — his world, his free world.

Eventually we felt that Quetico was enjoying his freedom, solitude, wild food, and a space that should satisfy any beaver. As the days went by and I travelled out to the bridge to watch, I often saw the head and the trailing wake that indicate a swimming beaver. One beaver. But beavers are family animals, and his sibling still lived in the rock pond at the education center, still on public display.

Serendipity is a word that has come into use in the English language relatively recently. When something extra special, something that is splendid beyond the ordinary in life happens, then it is a wonderful word to have. So, when once more the phone at the Sanctuary rang I listened to the request. Serendipity!

"Could you take the second beaver, too?"

"Yes!"

Her keepers brought her in a wire kennel. The beaver was fat and shiny but cranky. As she crouched in the cage, I wanted to tell her that her captivity was almost over, that in about an hour she would be swimming free with Quetico. That she would know him again, I did not doubt. So we put the kennel in the car and once more drove out Bear Cave Road to the edge of the wetland. There, we set the kennel on the shore facing the reeds and opened the door. The beaver did not hesitate. She was out into the reeds and into the water and away.

I do not know how long it took her to meet Quetico, nor what the meeting was like. Cautious? Glad? That the meeting did take place, I know, for during the long summer evenings as I watched I saw two heads and two silver Vs cutting the water.

All the long summer I watched those beavers. The old lodge was repaired. And as fall drew in, they began to store their winter food supply. I wanted to applaud wildly; these two beavers who had never been free, who had had no parents to teach them, knew exactly what to do. I saw fresh sticks on the lodge, and the green of freshly anchored branches around it until the ice came and the snow, and winter settled in.

I could not help wondering how the beavers would survive the winter, so as soon as the ice was away and the logging road passable, my dog and I went out to the wetland. We stood on the bridge and looked. The water was still and cold. The distant lodge looked to be in good repair, and though it seemed somewhat foolish, I called. "Quetico!"

For several moments I waited and then — a beaver coming straight towards the bridge! He came, turned and whacked his tail, so closely that the dog and I were splashed. But he wasn't finished. He swam under the bridge and splashed us from the other side. This splashing became a ritual greeting, not only that first season, but the second year and a third. As I write this, a bitterly cold January wind is whipping across Muskoka. Will there be a fourth season? For a wild beaver, Quetico is becoming elderly. But I hope so. Ours has been a fine friendship.

Life with Beavers

3

A BEAVER IN THE HOUSE

I live in a small house in a valley. Standing on a rise in the middle of the valley is a huge barn, brooding like a placid hen over the surrounding fields and woods. The barn, three times larger than the house, is home to assorted cats, raccoons, skunks, foxes, ducks, geese, a lion and an otter. The house has room for assorted cats, four dogs, a beaver, and me.

The house has an L-shaped living area, a bedroom, a bathroom, a tiny kitchen and a storage room. This part of the house sits more or less squarely on a fieldstone foundation. The huge stones were mined from the rock wall guarding the east side of the valley, and about one hundred years ago a beautiful log house was built firmly on this foundation. Unfortunately, one summer night some years ago the house burned to the ground.

As the number of inhabitants increased, I decided that the present house wasn't big enough, perhaps reasoning that if I could confine my artistic "messes" to a studio, the remainder of the house would stay more tidy. Thus, I hired a friendly neighbor, who, though somewhat given to clutching a beer bottle in one hand while he worked with the other, had managed to build his own family quite a nice house.

My studio is one step down from the living room, with lots of windows. However, my neighbor's attachment to the

Quibble helps to build the fence.

bottle had evidently grown stronger with time, because the studio's attachment to the house has become steadily weaker. And of course it does not have the advantage of a good fieldstone foundation. I can still plug the cracks with pink insulation, but the various developing entrances and exits provide an opportunity for wild creatures to make themselves at home. A couple of raccoons move freely between the ceiling and the roof, and in the springtime they can nest easily between the outside wall and the inside wallboard. (Though at one time the space was filled with insulation, that seems to have disappeared.) Every year I hear the soft whimpering of baby raccoons. Underneath the studio, which was built on concrete blocks and sturdy beams ("That's fine," I was assured), live a couple more raccoons, a few cats and at least two skunks. The skunks are friends of mine so I don't mind.

At one time the studio was actually used as a studio. At the far end, a big bay window is screened off as an aviary for birds — budgies, cockatiels, finches and a Roselle parakeet — all refugees brought by the Humane Society. The near end of the room, where it opens from the main house, is now shut off by a low, sturdy iron gate. An iron gate. The gate is the gift of Ralph, my Nova Scotian brother-in-law. Shortly after Ralph terminated (politely) a visit to my house, I received a phone call from the bus depot in Huntsville. A large, heavy, flat parcel had arrived for me from Nova Scotia. It was an iron gate, with a note from Ralph. "I did not really like being chased around the house by a beaver," the note read. "Possibly other guests don't either." In other words, when company arrived, I was to confine the resident beaver to the studio. Beavers chew wood. Iron might hold one, at least temporarily!

Witness the "arches" in my house. They are not the smoothly fashioned golden arches familiar on every continent the world around, but they are far more interesting. Each one is unique, carved personally by a beaver. The first arch was at the front door. Though doors may shut out dogs, cats, wolves, bears, even humans, to a beaver wooden doors are a mere temporary impediment. A beaver can chisel an archway at the bottom of a door — an archway large enough to let his fat self through — in about twenty minutes. However, since the cats and the raccoons also began to use the front-door archway, I covered the lower two feet of the door with tin. I liked the door. It was almost antique, with old-fashioned panels and trim, and a window of rather heavy old glass. The tin did not really add to its attractiveness, but it did deter the beaver for a few days. Then, with strong teeth and dextrous hands, he simply removed it. I have had to refer to this arch in the past tense, because it became necessary to replace the wooden door with a modern door of steel. But the other arches, for the most part, remain.

The kitchen has a half door, installed to keep the dogs out. For the dogs, it was sufficient; though they might stand up and peer over pathetically at the food, they could not come in. A beaver could. He simply settled down and applied himself to the lower right-hand corner. Grind, chew — presto, an entrance arch! However, the food (romaine lettuce, apples, yams) is generally safely stored in the refrigerator, with its impenetrable door. And though the door of the fridge is heavily scored with teeth marks, even a beaver cannot cut through. The floor-level cupboards, where dog kibble is stored, did not survive so well. Those cupboards were once lovely pine, handcrafted by a real artist. Now another craftsman has chiselled in his designs — deeply. The satin finish has disappeared to beaver height. The door corners no longer fit. They are either missing or curved, and if rounded corners do not fit square corners, so be it. That's life with a beaver!

Before the advent of the iron gate, I had tried, when company came, shutting the beaver in the bathroom. However, Quibble was most determined that no human should come into his territory; they were to be rousted out of the house as soon as possible. The first time I tried to lock him in the bathroom, I timed him. Twenty minutes! He was through and out. It wasn't that he didn't enjoy the bathroom, as for him it was rather a special place. The toilet seat was decorated with long teeth gouges, but the bathtub bore the most evidence of beaver work. During the winter, when the outdoor ponds are frozen, the bathtub is a great place for a beaver to swim, and Quibble seemed to quite enjoy the sound of his teeth grating against the white enamel. He managed to produce somewhat the same sound on the iron gate.

Would you like a tour of a house where beavers have lived? If nothing else, you would understand that beavers cannot be household pets. And a strong streak of insanity is likely a prerequisite to allowing one in. Consider the following examples.

I had to have the basement steps replaced. Quibble could go downstairs fast enough, but his ascent was inevitably slow because each stair had to be munched on. Down in the darkness at the bottom of the staircase, two steps had been completely consumed. And of course the door at the bottom, as predictably as McDonald's, had its archway. Quib had his home in the basement and needed an archway through which he could haul wood (from my wood-stove pile), blankets, laundry, books and any other furnishings he felt he required.

I have never been a great pianist, but at one time I was an acceptable piano player, and have always wanted a piano in the house. Without one, a home seemed incomplete. Even after a buck deer in rut managed to pierce its antler through my left hand and so lowered my abilities from "acceptable" to "only in private," I kept my piano. A lovely instrument, oak, with elaborately carved legs and mellow ivory keys, it was always slightly out of tune. But my playing had become of such a calibre that a slight flatness was not of major importance. I simply enjoyed the piano.

Some animals really like music. Many years ago, before the log house burned, a wild bear would come out of the woods and stay just beyond the creek. I believe he liked country-and-western music. Perhaps (here I am, being anthropomorphic) Quib really was a good critic and considered the sounds I made unworthy and offensive. However, the lovely scroll work on the piano legs caught his attention. He sat himself down to make it like absolutely no other scroll work in the world. He concentrated on the right leg. The long incisor cuts and cross indentation, from short nibbles made the leg remarkably original. Some months later, when it became absolutely necessary for me to sell the piano, the purchaser did not seem to realize the value of Quibble's contribution. He even hinted that a reduction in price would be suitable. I was offended. No more original piano leg exists anywhere in the entire world. The flatness could be remedied by a good piano tuner.

Generally, beavers like fresh wood. Dead wood may be used in construction, and I do wonder if antique wood is somehow attractive. From my mother's mother, Grandma Bannister, I inherited a cedar chest. Inheritance has not figured largely in my life — no fortune, no stately home — but a very special cedar chest. Grandma Bannister did not have much to leave. For as long as I had known her, she had been bedridden with arthritis. When she announced she was going to die, and did, I was only a child. To my older sister, she willed her bedroom suite, an elegant affair and by now likely designated an authentic antique. I cannot recall that she left anything at all to my younger sister. To me, she left the cedar chest.

A fine chest it is. Smooth, bordered with intricate design and (above everything) smelling richly of cedar. I remember the warm scent of her room. I remember the delight with which, when it became mine, I filled it with my collection of questionable treasures. I never anticipated its fate. For well over forty years it stood in my house, bordering on regal, always emitting the sweet smell of cedar.

Please begin to understand why Ralph felt an iron gate was a necessary part of my household. Quibble liked the smell of cedar. And so, one day when he was wandering alone in the house, he ambled down the step into the studio, sniffed the cedar, and decided to taste it. He gnawed all along the lid. He removed parts of the design. He adjusted the legs, each to its own height. And then, having initiated a new design in furniture, he left it. The overall theme of my house is not Early Canadian or Edwardian or Victorian. It is Original Canadian Beaver.

Beavers are very territorial beings; a particular swamp and the surrounding area is the family home. No trespassers are allowed — at least only selected neighbors. A bird might build its nest; that is temporary. A moose may come to the water to drink or wallow in the lily pads, or a deer, or a fox or a bear. None will be invited to stay. An unrelated beaver will often (not always!) be driven away. I regard it as rather a compliment to my friends that Quibble regarded them as beavers and asked them to leave.

In water, beavers swim swiftly and gracefully. On land, they look like slow, lumbering creatures; however, despite the plodding impression, beavers can run — and fast — either away from danger or towards a threat. They also have a limited ability to climb. In the house, any chair or bed is easily mounted: arms act as levers on top, and with a mighty heave of the tail, they're up. However, the dining room table is beyond reach.

A family from New York City was visiting for a summer vacation. To them, all animals were wonderful, as were the meadows and the trees, the rocks and the hills, and the vast expanse of the star-filled sky at night. The dogs, cats, raccoons, skunks and foxes were all part of the country adventure, as was Quibble. Papa, a native New Yorker, weighed well over three hundred pounds. For him to think of a beaver, that proud Canadian symbol, as aggressive — hardly!

One particular day, we had decided to visit the village, and were waiting outside by the car for Papa. Waiting and waiting. Finally, I went back into the house to find him, hands raised, standing in the middle of the dining room table, silent and helpless. Quibble, hands also up stretching as tall as he could, stood between the table and the door. Sometimes he charged towards the table and tried, as desperately as a beaver can, to reach up. It was a standoff!

I do not subscribe to all the beliefs of biologists, but they do say that the male beaver is more territorial, more aggressive than the female. If this is true, then Quibble was most certainly male. But perhaps Beaver was female. She was protective, but she did not actually attack.

The very first second in a remote lake.

Free!

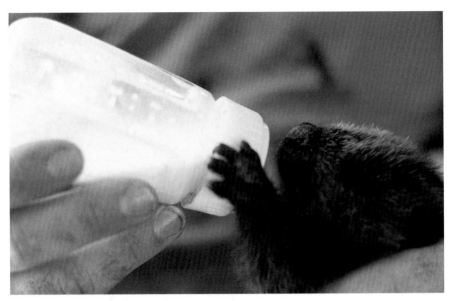

Beaver kits must be raised on a special formula.

Playtime in the pond.

A beaver named Earthquake — because he whacked his tail every time a human went near him — is set free.

Qualicum and Alix — friends, why not?

Carly — still unable to walk.

McGinty — did you ever see such a contented look on a beaver face?

*Beavers **love** mud!*

Beavers spend hours grooming themselves.

Casey — a small beaver who grew into a compassionate adult.

Little Beaver makes himself at home.

A beaver kit eats Pablum.

*Cassidy learns to take natural food —
here, raspberry cane and aspen leaves.*

Clancy. His tail was caught in a trap, froze, and had to be amputated.
He finally put on weight and could swim very well.

The cage door is open and it is time to go free —
a moment of hesitation.

For several weeks, two of my human friends came to the house every Wednesday night to make "mud pies," as our attempts at pottery were disrespectfully referred to by other friends. As long as I was in the house, Beaver accepted them philosophically. Evidently, I was regarded as head beaver. After all, we were playing with mud!

Now my friend Doreen Nowak's great-grandparents had cleared the valley and built the log house and the great barn, so if anyone had territorial rights to the area, she did. My other friend, Joan Charles, had grown up in England, where her family had run a pub, and she had become the wife of a rural rector in Rosseau. (I firmly believe the pub background should be a prerequisite for all clergy wives!) At that time, Doreen was building lovely clay pots, and Joan was constructing a Noah's Ark, complete with a multitude of almost-identifiable animals. The fact that a duck might be bigger than a bear bothered her not at all. We called it folk art, and it sold well at our little store. I cannot remember exactly what creation I was laboring over one particular evening. Beaver was asleep on the couch, and the phone rang. A bird (an owl, I think) had been hit by a car; could I please come and pick it up?

Of course. I did not think twice about leaving my friends with Beaver.

Later, however, Joan said, "Your car wasn't out of the driveway before she wanted us out."

Apparently she pushed. She tried to shift their chairs. She sniffed and huffed. She circled. Doreen had then suggested bribery. "She ate everything we gave her. I opened the fridge door. She went in," Joan explained. "She came out. I shut the kitchen gate — the arch."

Beaver was persistent.

Joan grabbed the broom, and Doreen opened the bathroom door. They swept the indignant beaver in. But of course, the door was wooden, the arch already begun. All Beaver had to do was make it a little larger! Luckily, her escape from the bathroom coincided with my return to the house, and once I was in, Beaver simply ambled back to the couch, heaved herself up, and went back to sleep.

Quibble, on the other hand, was more likely to accept other animals than humans into the house. Of all the dens built by wild creatures in the great wilderness, a well-built beaver lodge is one of the most impenetrable. Beavers are careful, thorough builders. Using mud and sticks, the occasional stone, and vast quantities of ingenuity, they carry their construction materials in their arms or their mouths. They pile and pack, arrange and rearrange, until the resulting lodge is so strong that a prowling wolf or predatory bear cannot penetrate it. Down inside, the beaver family is safe.

One enemy that might possibly invade, though, is the long, thin, meat-eating otter, who can swim up the entrance tunnel. Whether this happens often is a matter of biological debate. An otter could take a beaver kit. I can only say that Quibble did not (most definitely not!) like the only otter he ever met. Beavers may accept that human habitations are subject to all sorts of invasions, but for his own habitation Quibble set a limit, and that was, emphatically, no otters.

The event was quite natural. On Highway 69, north of Parry Sound, a truck ran over an otter and left it badly injured on the graveled shoulders of the road. Two men, more compassionate than the truck driver, stopped, saw that the otter was suffering and carefully lifted it into their car. Hoping that there was some way to help it, they drove the fifty miles to the Sanctuary. The injuries were extensive, and the otter died only a few minutes after they arrived. However, the men had thoroughly absorbed the odour of otter. One man, as they started back towards their car, stopped suddenly and frowned a bit.

"I hear you have a beaver in the house," he said. "Can we see it?"

I hesitated. I knew Quibble's fame was growing, but I also knew how he felt about extra humans in the house.

"Please?" he implored.

Who am I to discourage anyone who is really interested in beavers? I would stand firmly between them. I let the men in.

Bad decision. Quibble ignored me. He smelled otter. He charged.

His arms around one man's knee, huffing, his tail quivering, he pushed him right out the door. Both men left, politely, and I followed and managed to close the door before the irate beaver came out too.

But Quibble was not content. As we stood on the porch, discussing the attributes of beavers and otters, I heard a continual scratching and scraping, thumping and banging and huffing inside. Keeping my mind on the lingering conversation was difficult. Trying to indicate that I was anxious about the interior of my house, I kept my hand on the door knob and credited its slight quivering to my imagination. At last the men left, and I turned to go in. The door would not open.

Quibble, now weighing about forty pounds, had taken a heavy wooden armchair, pushed it across the floor, angled it back and wedged it tightly beneath the door knob. No one, not human and not otter-smelling humans especially, would be allowed to enter his house.

He finally let me crawl through a window. And, may I say, the iron gate never did confine him.

THE POND BEAVERS

Everyone, no doubt, would like to own lakefront property, to be able to sit in the long light of an evening and watch the rays of the setting sun glimmer across the wide water. To do so now on the Muskoka Lakes, one must almost be a millionaire. The *Seguin*, the tourist steamboat that plies the Muskoka Lakes during the busy summer months has, during the cruise, a running commentary that draws attention to the shoreline mansions (no, not "cottages" anymore) and reveals how many millions of dollars each cost. This is all a sad comedown for what was once a wonderful wilderness area.

Our valley, along a gravel back road, has so far escaped the advance of the human population. Our wolves, singing, are still answered once in a while by the song of wild wolves. Deer still move in the surrounding woods, and a bear still lives in a cave up on the hillside. The pond I had dug, where I had been able to help so many little beavers learn about swimming and diving and mud, has shrunk back to its original creek bed, and trickles once more into a little stream among the alder roots. However, I now have a small lake.

The lake is the gift of the beavers. From our initial efforts with the natural stream on the property, a pond had emerged. Now, beaver efforts have resulted in the small lake. This pond/lake has been enjoyed by many creatures.

I am glad that God can make use not merely of our abilities, but of our inabilities. God has built this entire Sanctuary, for creatures from the orphaned mice to the lion, on my inability to say "No" to a wild creature in need. It was because of this weakness that Donald, the duck, came to the Sanctuary.

Paloma Plant, head of the Wildlife Division of the Toronto Humane Society, phoned. She is well aware of my inabilities.

"Would you be able to take a duck?" she asked, not quite tentatively.

"A wild duck?"

She dodged. "A brown duck."

"A mallard?"

She confessed. "It's a domestic duck. But we can't keep it." Now she was talking more quickly.

"A trucker just brought it in. He's been driving around with it in the front seat of his truck for the last few months. But now it is big. His boss says he has to get rid of it."

At least I hesitated.

"We'll just have to put it down," she added.

And so the duck came to live at the Sanctuary — a big, brown duck with a white splash across the chest and an attitude problem. Unfortunately, we named it Donald. When Donald began to lay eggs, it was too late to change her name.

Winter was coming. In the barn, enclosures were being prepared for creatures who would not be able to endure the cold and who had to be kept over the winter. For such domestic rabbits as we had (again, that inability to say no), we had a large area with a deep earth floor, lots of hay, a couple of kennels, and a window for light. Deciding that the addition of a pond would make it suitable for Donald too, it ended up housing a couple of female rabbits and a female duck named Donald.

November came. Though the snow held back, the temperature fell, and ice skimmed the edge of the little creek.

The phone rang.

Humans who work with animals frequently seem to suffer from this inability to say "No." However the disability must be tempered with discretion, or else one might end up with a hundred cats and be unable to provide for them properly. Once the refusal to refuse exceeds one's ability not only to provide, but to provide very well, the disability becomes irresponsibility, and the animals involved will suffer. But Donald was not suffering!

That made perfectly clear, let me introduce a very good friend of mine who suffers from this same weakness. Shirley Morin lives in Trenton. For many years she was an agent for the Quinte Bay Humane Society. (Once she was given the "agent of the year" award for her work.) She cares about animals and she understands the provincial laws that relate to them. She knows that very, very few laws do anything to protect beavers, and she had come across two beavers who were in desperate need. Hence the phone call.

Dozens of horses and cattle, goats and sheep owed their lives to Shirley's intervention. Literally hundreds of dogs and cats had been rescued from horrendous situations because Shirley found them and fought for their rights to good and healthy lives. That was her job. But beyond that, Shirley cares about wildlife. Her house is full of baby birds and squirrels, chipmunks and raccoons, all being given needed care. All on their way back to wild lives.

So she was not surprised when she was asked to intervene on behalf of two beavers. Nor was I surprised when her call came through.

"Two beavers," she announced over the phone. (Shirley frequently forgets to say "Hello.") "The county is draining wetlands — for roads. Two beavers have been driven out. If I get them, you'll take them in, of course."

Not really a question. Shirley knows how welcome beavers are at Aspen Valley. The following is her story:

> In late November 1996, when I arrived at work, Shelter Supervisor Leslie Chapman asked me to phone a woman in Prince Edward County who was concerned about two young beavers who had taken up residence in the side of a drainage ditch. It seemed the beavers had followed a drain cut into a swamp between Highway 62 and the Bay of Quinte to their present location. The woman said the cost of removal was not a problem and that she would gladly assume any charges.
>
> As agents with the Quinte Humane Society, Leslie and I had removed an assortment of various animals — cats, dogs, horses, etc. But never beavers. We checked out the situation and admitted it was beyond our abilities. I contacted Animal Control for Belleville, which runs a pest-control business and does trapping. He paid the beavers a visit and said, "No problem." But it would cost.
>
> One hundred and fifty dollars each. The woman refused to pay for even one beaver.
>
> Leslie and I decided it was now up to us to rescue the beavers. After considerable discussion and haggling, the animal-control man lowered the price and I agreed to pay. A few days later, he turned up at the shelter with the beavers, which he said were yearlings.
>
> In the meantime, I had contacted Audrey Tournay for advice on how to care for these animals until we could transport them to her establishment. She gave us the wisdom of her experience, and a stall in our barn was set up with bedding, food and plenty of water. Every few days they were given aspen branches to supplement their diet.

Leslie and I discussed the transporting of the beavers and decided that, weather permitting, we would go on her first day off. Once again, the control officer and Audrey came to our aid and told us how to get the beavers into a cage for transport. We got on each side of the beavers with pieces of plywood and made a hallway for them into the cage. Every step of the way they complained with a murmuring sound.

The night before we left there was a snow storm, and we had heard that sections of Highway 12 were closed so we headed north on 62 and on through Algonquin Park. Up to the park the roads had been plowed bare, but the roads in the park, although plowed, were snow-covered and slippery in spots. However, our guardian angels were looking after us, and we arrived safely at Aspen Valley. On our return trip south the plows had opened Highway 12, so we were able to travel our usual route south.

The two beavers who arrived in the cage in the back of Shirley's station wagon were very cranky beavers, and they had every right to be. Somewhere near Belleville, out in a wetland, they had built and prepared their lodge, safe and warm against the onslaught of cold and snow. They had cut and stored a sufficient supply of poplar, aspen and birch so that they would eat well beneath the ice. When humans had wantonly destroyed their habitat, left them to starve until they were trapped and caged, and finally driven them miles and miles in a vehicle which, to them, would have been intolerably noisy and smelly, they became distinctly unhappy. When the cage was carried into the barn, the beavers huffed and their tails quivered in indignation.

More friends for Donald! Although at first all the duck would know was that her pond had been replaced with one bigger and deeper.

Over the years at the Sanctuary, we have watched some curious friendships. That dogs and cats are often good friends was no surprise. Laddie, our border collie, was for a period of some years friends with a wild coyote. Skunks also seem to be very adaptable, with skunk–dog friendships, skunk–raccoon ones and, just now, one between a wild skunk and our lion. Quibble had had to share his house with several bear cubs, and as long as they did not trespass into his particular space, he nonchalantly accepted them. He had a little more trouble with a small black kitten who seemed to confuse him continually with her mother. He would pick the kitten up in his arms, carry it across the room and stuff it into a corner. Eventually the kitten learned to hang limp and stay in the corner until the beaver waddled away. Perhaps that was not really friendship! But now, two wild beavers were being asked to accept captivity with a domestic duck.

They learned. The beavers took the aspen we brought them (by the van load), ate some and with the rest constructed a fairly proper beaver lodge with an entrance tunnel and easy access to the pond. Satisfied, they moved in. So did Donald.

They tried ignoring her. They did not, at first, mind sharing the pond. They even shared their food. Donald ignored the aspen and the apples, yams and peas. But the bananas! Donald loved bananas.

Perhaps the beavers knew that, when they were finally returned to the wild, no amount of searching would produce anything like a banana tree, so that fruit could be relegated exclusively to the duck. Perhaps that victory gave Donald courage. At any rate, she decided to become the pond boss. There the beavers would be in the water, lazing away the long winter days, when Donald, squawking and pecking, attacked. When she had succeeded in driving them out, she would dive and preen and chuckle to herself.

She took the bananas. She commandeered the pond. And then Donald moved into the beaver lodge. She began by allowing only one beaver inside at a time. Quacking hysterically, flapping her wings to create minor hurricanes, she would drive the other beaver to a dark corner across the enclosure. There it would huddle, muttering, waiting — maybe trying to devise a plan. Surely wild-living beavers never had to deal with a duck like Donald.

Swimming in the pond some months after their release.

Finally, the resolution was quite simple. For all her flurry, Donald did not weigh nearly as much as one ponderous beaver, and they simply ignored her and lumbered into their den. Like two small mountains, they hunched, immovable. Donald had to sleep beside them or (occasionally) between them. For an entire winter, the lodge was inhabited by a reluctant threesome.

When spring showed the first signs of coming, when the first crows came back from the city, Donald began to lay eggs. Eggs in the beaver lodge! How could two dignified beavers contend with duck eggs in their lodge? There was nothing to do . . . except sit on them. Which they did. (We could not help speculating about what went on in the darkness of that beaver-duck lodge. Should we let Donald try to hatch one egg, just to see . . .?)

To a wild animal in captivity, stress can be as dangerous as disease. The stress the beavers began to show could not, seriously, be attributed to Donald. They had been raised free. They had lived free. And for almost four months they had been in the dim, warm safety of the barn. But now, outside, spring had begun to come, and even confined in as ideal a location as possible, the beavers felt the soft, new season beginning; snow was melting. Even from the barn, they could hear the running water of the creek. Deep in the bottom of the outside pond, green weeds were beginning to grow. The beavers were impatient for freedom. They huffed. Their tails quivered with anger. We had little choice. If we kept them confined, they would die. If we gave them their freedom, being experienced in the wild, they would have a good chance of survival. They would certainly not miss Donald!

Roads, made impassable by mud, prevented us from taking them to a more remote location, so we decided we could release them in our creek. They would then find their way down with the flow of the water to the river and the little lakes and there be free to choose their own home.

What had once been the island in the pond was now surrounded on two sides by mud, on the third by the trickle of the creek and on the fourth by a deep pond. On the island, the tamaracks still stood, green and tall. Alders grew thickly at the pond end. Though the water supply was minimal, the mud supply was enough to satisfy any beaver.

We carried the beavers in kennels down to the edge of the pond and opened the doors. The beavers did not hesitate. Out into the water they swam together, then they swam apart. They swam as silently, as grace-fully as only wild beavers can. They pulled themselves up on the island and groomed themselves and then each other, carefully, and swam again. For a long while I watched them, and then, wishing them a long, free and contented life, left them there. I could do nothing more for them.

I expected that, during the night, the beavers would make their way down the creek. However, in the morning they were side by side on the island, asleep in the warmth of the rising sun. We did not offer them food — wild beavers know where to find food for themselves.

The next morning the beavers were still on the island, and the next, and the next. They began to work. They cut alder. They carried mud. On the island, first they built a small lodge beneath the tamaracks and then, having inspected the little dam we had built and finding it sadly inadequate, they began to construct a dam of their own. The water rose slowly. More sticks. More mud. The water rose. The island grew smaller. More sticks. More mud. They built their lodge bigger. Night after night they worked. Water rose and began to flow around the end of the dam. The beavers lengthened it. The water rose. The island disappeared. All spring and summer they worked. Eventually, the dam was about one hundred feet long. A lake grew — small, but a lake! Lakefront property in Muskoka!

All summer they continued to work. When fall came, they collected the aspen and alder for their winter food supply, anchored it beside their lodge, and piled up more mud. The water froze, and snow covered Muskoka. Inside the lodge and under the ice, the beavers were no doubt sleepily active. Tracks in the snow showed where, during the long nights, coyotes and wolves investigated the lodge.

When another spring arrived, the beavers did not wait for all the ice to melt. As soon as an ice-free hole appeared, they came out and cut fresh saplings. The beavers had come to stay.

We loved having the beavers and the little lake they had made. But we also knew that when a good food supply is not available, beavers will move on. The first year the beavers went through the culvert under the road and cut the smaller trees from a large stand of aspen. Because the supply was not infinite and because we did not want the animals endangered if they decided to drag larger branches not through the culvert, but across the road, we supplemented the food supply by leaving cut branches in the field beside the pond. A friend, who is steadily clearing one of his lots, has brought several truckloads of aspen every fall. Maybe the beavers stay because they feel they have reached some sort of heaven; we like to think they stay because they like us.

75

The tamaracks were the only victims. As the lake deepened and the water covered the island, the trees died.

The second spring when heavy construction on the dam was finished and the pond was a fair way along to becoming our larger lake, only one beaver seemed to be at work, endlessly pulling branches into the water. One beaver grazing among the cattails or munching on the green sprouts in the meadow. Were we seeing the same beaver all the time or were they taking turns doing all the work? Half the summer passed before we really understood: one large beaver, and then the second, and, one quiet summer evening just outside the lodge, two more very small beavers.

Over the years the beaver family has grown. Away down the creek, where it flows through the swamp, is another small pond with a little round island. If these beavers follow the same pattern, some of them will likely establish a home there. I hope so!

Neighborhoods vary. Mine is wonderful. In the evening, I can look out of my window and see the shimmering silver V of beavers swimming on the water. Even the dead tamaracks are beautiful, laced with ice in the wintertime.

DO BEAVERS LAUGH?

"Hamish," I called across the water to my long-legged Labrador, "that beaver is teasing you!"

It was. I don't believe that the serious considerations of surviving in the wilderness have ever deprived beavers of their sense of fun. I was having a quiet evening on the shore of a small horseshoe bay in a quiet section of Lake Rosseau. No other humans were around. The dog was paddling in the water along the shore.

Then a beaver swam around the point and into the bay.

Hamish's head went up. His nostrils quivered. For one moment the beaver was still, and then he slapped his tail. Hamish dove into the deep water — the chase was on!

Hamish headed towards the rings of water the whacking tail had left. The beaver dove too, smoothly under the water and was gone. By the time the dog had arrived at the splash point, the beaver had surfaced at the other side of the bay, where he whacked his tail again. Hamish swivelled around and headed for the beaver. The beaver dove. By the time Hamish had reached the second splash point, the beaver was back at the first and whacked his tail again. Back and forth they went, back and forth and back and forth. The beaver was having a wonderful time. After about half an hour, Hamish was completely exhausted and came to shore. With a farewell whack, the beaver disappeared around the point of land.

Beavers play among themselves. They wrestle, arms on each other's shoulders, feet against the other's chest, they push. The object seems to be to topple your adversary backwards, sideways or simply down. The escape is to dodge under the other fellow's arm when you can. The teeth, which could be dangerous weapons if the fight were serious, do not come into play at all.

Lacking any other beaver to play with, Quibble often chose me as his partner. When he was small, I needed only one hand as an appropriate opponent. But to make the competition fair, I had to sit on the floor. He was very strong. Gripping my hand with both of his and pressing it against his chest, he would push, grunt and twist until I gave way. Then he would retain his grip on my hand until he exerted sufficient pressure to resume the game. If he wanted to play and I was busy with something else and ignoring his wishes, he would tackle my leg, usually about knee height. He would wrap his arms around my leg and with his cheek applying pressure, push!

When Quibble was a full-grown beaver, I did not necessarily win the push games.

To explain why I might reasonably panic if I lost sight of one of the beavers, I must explain that our road is a dead-end road with very little traffic, but it runs close to the beaver pond. One spring, having two very wild beavers who needed a quick release, I allowed them into the pond. I felt that they would follow the stream down to the river, and then they would have their choice of a hundred Muskoka lakes. One beaver did head towards the river. The other, for reasons unknown, headed up the road towards trouble. I knew he was heading for an area of unfriendly humans and a busier road — either of which could mean death.

Beavers can move over land very, very quickly. I ran ahead of him and tried to turn him back, but he dodged me, one side of the road to the other, back and forth. He would not turn. With a heavy branch, I tried to push him. Mistake! Like the rodent he was, he leapt at me, his teeth slashing my leg. With a final run, he ran into the bush in the general direction of the stream. I'm not sure who actually won that round, but as I wiped the blood from my leg, I did grin a little. The beaver was running away from the danger area!

Beavers like companionship, and I like the companionship of beavers. So, on warm summer afternoons, Quibble and I often swam together in the deeper end of the pond. Although only one end was deep enough for me, the entire pond was deep enough for Quibble. He would swim in circles around me, then whip around the island and do a fast swim-by. Sometimes, he would linger quietly beside me while I swam, as though waiting for my attention to wander. And then he would disappear. Gone, completely gone. I would call — no answering grunt — and call again. But not a ripple. Nothing, but one absolutely vanished beaver.

At that point, I would think of the road. Usually I did not really panic until after about five or six minutes. Then, growing more frantic, I would wade around the island and search in the cattails. If I were really desperate, I would range up through the fields, calling. I never got an answer. Hot, worried, envisioning Quib, unsuspecting, wandering up the road, I would consider going back to the house, getting my car and frantically following him. But to do that I had to swim across the water.

Still no sound, no ripple, no beaver. Suddenly, a hard nose would jab into my back, with a flurry of water as Quib whipped out of range and surfaced, watching me with laughter in his eyes. Believe me — laughter! Poking me in my back became one of his favorite games.

I hold the Bible in deep respect. The stories in it range from tales of horrible cruelty, as in the tails of foxes set on fire to burn the crops of the Philistines, to statements of deep, deep compassion, wherein God watches the smallest of sparrows. A very conservative theologian once explained to me that the principal difference between humans and animals is that humans are capable of compassion and of humor; animals, he stated, are not. Perhaps it is because the stories in the Scriptures arise from cultures very different from ours that we fail to recognize any humor in them.

Certainly, even in different human cultures, ideas of humor vary widely. To say that because we do not recognize humor in animals, therefore it does not exist is somewhat arrogant. To state that animals do not understand compassion is even more so. From long personal experience, I know animals enjoy humor; they also show compassion.

I will concede that no one can keep an accurate record of my dogs. The house is always home to several. Generally they arrive as strays and stay until they die of old age.

Hamish was a big, black dog, probably mostly Labrador retriever, with enough of some sort of hound to give him longer ears and long legs. He and I together had raised my first litter of baby raccoons. Those first four raccoons, named Pip, Merry, Sadie and Little, were about a week old when they arrived. Raising them was a great deal of work, which I shared with the dogs.

Hamish, especially, was intensely interested in them. He let them snuggle close to his belly, where they felt the sort of animal warmth their mother had not lived to give them. His big tongue (being considerably larger than a raccoon's tongue) seemed too rough for them, but he tried to bathe them. As they grew, Hamish seemed to develop a special friendship with Merry, the most dominant female. Only he knew why he preferred her to the others. When winter came, the four raccoons wandered off into the bush, to reappear, fit and fine, in the spring. Merry and Hamish resumed their friendship.

Somewhere in the bush across the road (then only a dirt road), Merry had her babies. At about six o'clock every evening she appeared up the driveway, and she and Hamish shared a bowl of kibble. Sometimes Hamish wandered with her off into the bush, but since he was free to go where he wanted (the days of no neighbors), I did not notice much and certainly did not worry.

One evening Merry did not come. Not that evening, nor the next. And though I felt that she was free to do as she pleased, Hamish seemed slightly agitated. By the fourth day of her non-appearance, he came to me, poked me with his nose and, stopping to look back at me, trotted down the laneway. Obviously, I was to follow him into the bush.

Hamish took me across a soggy ditch, through a stand of aspen, and up a hill to Merry. She had caught her neck between two saplings and was dead. But her four babies were alive. Hamish nosed them and looked at me. When I picked them up and started back through the bush towards the house, he followed, trotting happily.

Because Merry's babies had starved so long, only one survived: Freddy. Freddy was not a strong raccoon, and all winter when he had bouts of sickness Hamish stayed close beside him. He kept the other dogs away. When spring finally came and Freddy was ready to go free, Hamish made no protest. He turned his interest to other things.

Raccoons live everywhere — in cities, on farms, in wood boxes, in downtown cities amidst the skyscrapers, and in the deep woods where they never see a human being. (Perhaps the latter are the most fortunate of raccoons.) However, they are wild creatures and should not be compelled to be housepets.

Moon, a Toronto-born raccoon, began very early in his life to be more than that. He was mascot for a rock band and was taken all over Ontario. Before those genes that would finally draw him to the wilderness became active, he was relatively content with the company of humans and dogs — too content for his own safety. When, in September, Moon finally came to the Sanctuary, he was not sure about roaming free; he spent too much time sitting on the doorstep. I finally did what I do not do now. I opened the door and let him in.

So, he entered our family: three large, black Labrador retrievers, Kate, Abby and Duncan (Hamish had succumbed to old age); a rather fat, de-scented skunk named Donnelly; and me. I was not guilty of de-scenting Donnelly. However, because he had been de-scented before he was given to the Sanctuary, he could never go free. He had the run of the house and chose Duncan as his friend. When Moon arrived, they formed a contented trio. Only Moon was allowed to roam free, and I hoped he would want to go and live wild.

Donnelly and Duncan were good friends. Duncan slept on the couch, and Donnelly slept on top of him, both of them warm and content. Sometimes, in the cold of winter, Donnelly slept under the wood stove; Duncan, of course, did not fit. That first fall, Moon wandered freely in the bush. Sometimes days passed and we would not see him, but because that was the usual pattern for raccoons learning to be free, I was not concerned. If he continued to follow that pattern, the time would come when I would have only occasional glimpses of him along the edge of the woods, and then he would disappear altogether. Moon, however, had his own agenda.

When the first major blizzard whirled out of the north, Moon was at the door, scratching to be let in. (This was a pattern he followed for about four years. I might not see him for months, but the first blizzard would bring him in.) Of course I opened the door and in he came to spend the winter, ignoring Kate and Abby, accepting Duncan but curled up asleep with Donnelly. He fit under the wood stove.

My single life was filled with the pitter patter of little feet — dogs, skunk and raccoon. The skunk and raccoon ate together, slept together, and played together. I have found no record of such a friendship occurring in the wonderful wild, which does not for one moment mean that such friendships do not occur!

One evening, having travelled through darkness and driving snow, I arrived home. I was tired. The dogs greeted me. Moon was pacing the hall, and I presumed Donnelly was sleeping somewhere. So I lit the fire in the wood stove, had a cup of coffee and listened to the storm howling down the valley, battering at the windows. The house was wonderfully warm.

Moon continued to pace. Though it seemed strange, I thought he probably wanted out, so I opened the door. The storm whirled in. Moon did not want out. He continued to pace, pause and stare at me, and pace, up and down the hall, from door to window, up to my chair — no resting. The dogs, even Duncan, slept.

Finally, exasperated, I noticed that Moon was pausing at the back door. So he was being fussy and choosing which door he wanted out! Once again I opened a door and once again the storm swept in. Then I saw on the step, huddled from the cold and covered in snow, a shivering skunk. I lifted him in. He was so cold, Moon scampered back into the house, almost tumbling over himself in his joy. Donnelly was safe! I put a bowl of kibble on the floor by the fire. They ate together and then, satisfied, raccoon and thawing skunk curled up on the couch and slept.

While the dedicated scientific mind is explaining that incident, reluctant to concede that perhaps Moon really cared about Donnelly, I will rush on to another story from another time. And, before the obvious is tossed in as an explanation for this, I will tell you that I know border collies will herd almost anything. Laddy, my collie cross, had come out of the bush as a stray, but some instinct towards herding was quite evident in him. One neighbor kept sheep who sometimes wandered down the road to the Sanctuary. Laddy did not need instructions. He would see the sheep and instantly herd them back to where they belonged.

Laddy was a friendly dog, never aggressive to the wild creatures in the Sanctuary. He was tolerant of Quibble. He walked in the woods with deer and me, with bear cubs and me. He rather liked baby skunks and raccoons. Perhaps one of his best friends was a wild coyote. The coyote would simply appear at the upper end of the meadow that slopes between the hill and the house and stare down until Laddy trotted up to join her. For a while, they would disappear into the bush, and then I would see them, stretched out on the rocks sleeping in the sunshine. That relationship continued for several years and is likely not unique in the annals of dogdom. The fact that Laddy was neutered and their relationship was constant, not seasonal, meant no mating could have been involved.

We had a totally blind raccoon, named, with an exquisite lack of originality, Bandit. Bandit had been born blind and kept by someone in the city until his hormones kicked in and he became aggressive. Since his blindness made him unlikely to survive in the wild, we built him a large enclosure with hollow logs, a pool and an evergreen tree. There he lived in what we took to be contentment for a good number of years.

I never noticed Laddy paying any special attention to him, but one morning when I went out for an early morning visit with the animals, I found that Bandit had gone. I still do not know how he managed to escape from his enclosure. The "Why?" might not be so difficult. Even a blind raccoon would not necessarily lose the compelling curiosity that lands so many inquisitive raccoons in trouble. For years, Bandit had been hearing the sounds of the wilderness, smelling the scent of many curious things.

Bandit was somewhere out there, and he would not survive. The decision is always difficult: should we let him enjoy the few days of freedom before his inevitable death? Would he experience joy or terror? Should we begin an intensive search? If so, where in all the miles of bush would one begin? We did try. But after four days we abandoned the search and simply hoped he was happy and would not suffer much or for long.

Then one evening, after a long, warm day, I was sitting on the veranda. All the creatures were fed and watered. Such nursing care as was necessary was temporarily finished, so I drew a deep breath, leaned back in the chair, relaxed, and noticed Laddy, nose down, moving slowly up the back field — quite slowly. I called him but he ignored me.

Those herding instincts may be strong, even in a collie cross. But to use those instincts to herd straying, blind raccoons? Laddy had found Bandit somewhere out in the bush and brought him all the way home. Bandit lived contentedly in his enclosure for many more years.

Quibble was a contemporary of Duncan. Dogs have always been my favorite house friends, and I was glad of the acceptance and companionship that existed between the various beavers who have lived at the Sanctuary and the assorted dogs. Quibble shared our house willingly enough, but he tended to dominate the dogs. Beavers are family animals, living with parents, siblings, aunts and uncles with apparent affection. Quibble adopted all of us.

My memories of the Second World War are not closely connected with the tremendous suffering that occurred; principally I remember being told to be quiet at the dinner table so my father could hear radio announcer Jim Hunter and the latest war news. I remember, when peace was finally declared, thinking, "I wonder what it is like to live in a world with no war." Unfortunately, I still wonder.

Still, war has left its mark, even on those of us whose experience of it is quite remote. Everyone will remember the tremendous tension when the Gulf War began. Perhaps television had brought the reality tearing into our homes. I sat in the armchair and watched the glare of rockets, live, over Baghdad. And I thought of the terror and death being experienced at that very moment by human beings. I was remembering horrible things about war, memories I did not know I had — horrific events from books I had read, history I had studied. War. I gripped the arms of the chair as I watched the pictures on the television. I heard the sounds of guns and bombs.

I did not hear the approach of shuffling feet, but quietly two hands were placed on my knees, and, with a thrust from the great tail, Quibble was on my lap. Then his hands were on my shoulders, his head against my cheek and his big, warm body offering all the comfort it could. Had Quibble felt my tension? I think so.

Quibble demonstrated that same sensitivity again. One morning, long before dawn, word had come through that a very good friend of mine, Pat Swift, had died. Cancer had taken her from her husband, four young children, her friends and a world that needed her. I was angry and numb with grief, demanding "Why?" of an unanswering God. Then, once again, I felt those strong hands on my knees, the powerful push as Quib came up to me, his hands on my shoulders, his nose pushing at my cheek, his great warm body against me. God provided no answer . . . only a friend.

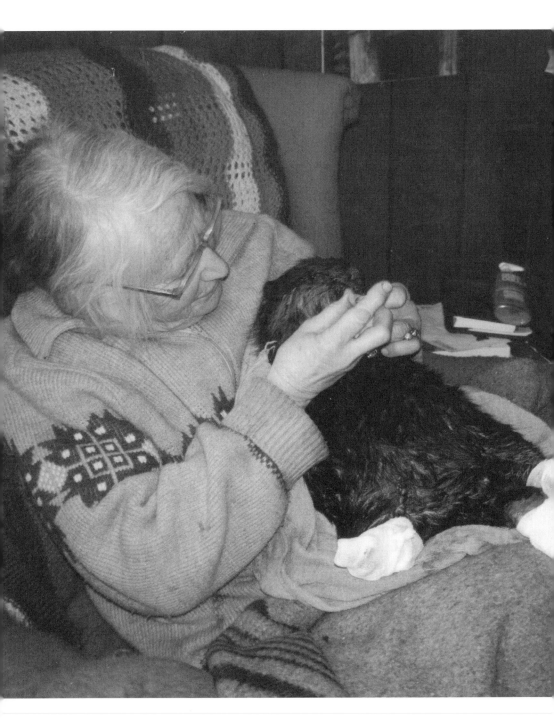

Beavers as Wildlife Ambassadors

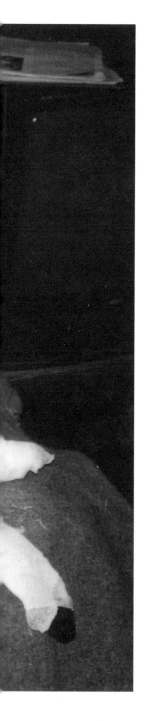

BEAVERS AS EDUCATORS

Beavers are great talkers. They talk to each other. Sometimes they mutter to themselves. When they are angry, they huff mightily. If they are involved in heavy work, they grunt. I cannot find a word to describe their everyday talk — it is neither a whine nor a whimper — both of which have unfortunate connotations. By the sound a beaver makes, its mood is easily interpreted. Rapid and high-pitched sound denotes anxiety. A rhythmic, quiet rise and fall is simply conversation. Sometimes, at the end of each "sentence," the tone will be raised as though a question is being asked, a conversation carried on. The beaver will pause for an answer and, once answered, continue talking.

The topic of such conversation may be unknown to us, but the mood is not. Most of it is friendly, companionable. If the beaver is excited, it may be emphasized by clenched fists or by hand movements, with outstretched fingers and arms. An angry beaver's head will be low, breathing heavy and tail quivering, beating a tattoo as the anger increases.

I am quite sure that the ability of the beaver to communicate with other beavers and even with other

Cody, for whom this book was written.

animals is one of the contributing factors to the legend that once upon a time humans and beavers could talk together.

I had taught school for over twenty-five years, and when I took early retirement and walked out of the school that last day, I thought I had left the classroom behind forever and ever. Now my life would be with raccoon kits and squirrels, little skunks, foxes and beavers. But then, beaver on my knee, I was back in the schoolroom. The subject this time was not English or history, and I was not the teacher. The beaver was. And he had a huge job ahead of him.

The hunting and trapping tradition was dominant in the Muskoka–Parry Sound districts, and quite frankly I wanted our woods and wetlands and meadows to be safe places for our wildlife.

The likelihood of changing the minds of parents was minimal, but children could learn. This teaching was not indoctrination. If the children could meet, see, even touch a wild creature, they would begin to understand that creatures have value beyond the economic, that they have a rightful place in our world, and that each animal is a living being — not owned, not subjugated, not inferior to us in any way. I was careful never to leave the impression that the wild animal making the public appearance, be it wolf, skunk, bear cub or beaver, was a "pet." To me, the word pet implies that I am keeping the animal in captivity, subject to me, for my own pleasure or convenience. The wild animals that I have known have been my friends.

One day, I did blow my cool. A man actually wanted to buy Quibble! But any buying, selling or trading of animals results in considerable stress on the animals involved.

"I need a beaver," he explained. "I've got a place up north where people come to take pictures. But I haven't got a beaver, and I need a pretty tame one, and," he added, looking out across the valley, "I hear you have some wolves. I could use them too. How much do you want for them?" The man managed to escape alive.

Buying and selling animals born outside of Ontario is not illegal.

The history of some of the wolves I've known is very sad. For two of them, the papers from the zoo from which they were rescued tells the story.

> "Female wolf, acquired from ————— in exchange for two lion cubs."
>
> "Female wolf, acquired from Alberta — her parents obtained from Indian, now deceased, Squanta Lake, Yukon."
>
> "Male wolf, given to —————, manager of 1000 Islands Wildlife Kingdom, by —————, as a gift, having been friends for many years."

Wolves are family-oriented creatures. Does it matter that they are torn out of these family groups? Would you like this?

Beavers are just as strongly family oriented as wolves. Quibble has taught many, many people a great deal about his species. More than that, he has been a fantastic companion and a very real friend. Family. Sell Quibble? There is just not enough money in the entire universe!

Some years ago, while at a Sanctuary display in Huntsville, a tourist from Europe saw a beaver for the first time. He was charmed and intrigued. That, I thoroughly understood. So he offered a hundred dollars to buy him, and then the beaver could fly to Europe. Politely I refused. He raised the offer to three hundred dollars. I refused once again, adding firmly that the beaver was not for sale. Perhaps he thought I was bartering, so, slightly exasperated, he asked, "How much?"

"Not all the money in the world," I replied. The tourist walked away, hands in his pockets, laughing.

No matter what animal or bird I take into a schoolroom with me, the reaction of both teachers and students is always interesting. Skunks create startled, rather frantic reactions. Because the animal is generally carried in a small kennel, the children at their desks or sitting in a circle on the floor never know exactly what animal to expect. Though they cannot detect an odor until they see the skunk, when I lift it out, they will instantly say "Whew!" and cover their noses.

My favorite moment is when, almost without exception, the worried teacher, fantasizing a dozen dreadful, smelly disasters, will say hurriedly: "But it is de-scented, isn't it?"

"No," I reply, and the panic never completely vanishes. Skunks are quite polite, though, and we have never had a spraying episode.

Different animals provoke different reactions. For a wolf pup or coyote pup it's, "Won't he bite?" For a porcupine, "Won't he throw his quills?" For a woodchuck, "Is that a beaver?" For a beaver, "Can we see his tail?"

Every reaction makes the need for education more evident. And the children begin to think. A Grade Five student wrote: "I really enjoyed seeing Swampy. It's quite a surprise. My Dad does not like beavers. He would rather trap them all. Well, I guess in some cases he is right but certainly Swampy . . . is not the kind of beaver you would trap and kill. Yours truly, Randy."

A trappers' association was gathering in the little town of Minden. There was much publicity, with coverage in the newspapers and radio and television. Pictures of pelts of hundreds of dead animals were displayed. Following all this, I had an urgent telephone call from a nursery school. Would I bring a beaver over so the little children could meet him?

Unaware of the reason for the teacher's urgent request for our presence, we made the trip to Minden. I carried the very alive beaver into a small nursery school, where little children sat on the floor in a circle, eagerly waiting. Beaver on my knee, I sat in the circle too. I talked. The beaver talked more than I did, quietly, continually. The children listened and giggled. They squirmed. Beaver squirmed. I put him on the floor. He walked around, visiting the children, sometimes standing on his haunches to peer at them more closely, maintaining a soft, nosey conversation.

After the children had patted him and heard him talk, and it was all over, the teacher handed me a copy of the local newspaper. On the front page, a large picture featured one of those nursery children, sitting in the midst of a pile of beaver pelts, not quite smiling. The picture was entitled, "Future Trapper!"

Would the remembered touch of the hand of a live, warm beaver foster a doubt about killing in the mind of the child? Simply by being just themselves, beavers never fail to impress. I usually sit with the beaver on my knee, on a desk, or (if the children are on the floor) on a low chair or even on the floor with them. I want each child to be able to see the animal clearly, and if the animal is willing, even let each child touch it.

The children are asked to be quiet. Then the soft squeal of a delighted child is heard: "Oh! I touched a skunk! ""I touched a porcupine!" "I touched a beaver," indicating a new attitude beginning to form.

When I have a beaver, I talk to the children about their anatomy, showing how perfectly they are made for the life they lead: the front feet like five-fingered hands for carrying, the back feet webbed for swimming strongly, tiny eyes that can stay open under water because of a fine transparent film covering them, ears and nostrils that close tightly. The teeth, long and orange, always fascinate, and behind those great teeth a flap of skin that can close to keep out water when the beaver is swimming and carrying sticks. Sometimes I can induce the beaver to groom, and the children learn how oil is secreted from a gland at the base of the tail to keep them dry, then combed through all the fur with a split claw on each back foot, just perfect for the purpose. However, always the greatest beaver wonder is the tail — broad and heavy, like fat leather.

After every visit, the children write a letter like this one:

Thank you for coming into our class. I really liked it a lot. I think the beaver is the nicest beaver I have ever seen. I really enjoyed what you showed us and I thought it was interesting. I hope you can come back again sometime. The best I liked is when we got to touch the beaver and I thought the tail felt weird.

Yours truly, Kristi

We visit nursery schools, elementary schools, high schools, camps, scout troops and girl guide companies — anywhere we feel that humans will appreciate the wonder of wild things. We've even been to camps for senior citizens.

I usually try to be good. However, to one very sophisticated senior's camp to which I was invited, I took not a beaver but a very lovely little skunk. Her name was Blossom. She was quite accustomed to visiting schools and, despite the fact that she was not de-scented, had never caused any problem. After all, she had always been treated with perfect politeness. As she sat quietly and beautifully on my knee, a tall, well-coiffed woman came upon us. Her perfectly made-up face contorted with horror, and she raised two beautifully manicured hands to her mouth:

"A skunk!" she cried. "Oh, my God."

I tickled Blossom's neck just a little. "Oh, Blossom," I said. "She likes you. She thinks you are God!"

The lady, not amused, stalked away, head high. Perhaps Blossom was amused.

After a visit to another camp for seniors, Beaver became ill. We had been really busy visiting schools and camps, but when he became lethargic and refused to eat or even drag the laundry around the house, I knew he was indeed unwell and needed a visit to the veterinarian's office. While the veterinarian was making an anxious examination, I gave an account of our visit with the seniors. After my description of that visit, the veterinarian's nine-year-old daughter, watching and listening, came up with the reason for Beaver's problem.

The camp where Beaver and I had been was an escape for nice ladies from the city. They were anxious to meet a little of the wilderness so that when they returned to their apartments or neat suburban houses, they could remember that forests and meadows, streams and lakes and beavers still exist. Beaver and I had talked to them about beavers, and Beaver had allowed them to look at him and see how wonderfully God had made him. When that part was over, I took the women for a hike out through the woods to a large wetland, where I showed them a beaver lodge and dam and explained how necessary beavers are to the wilderness. Back at the camp, one lovely lady gathered her fragile courage to actually touch Beaver. And she murmured covetously, "My, how I would like a beaver-skin coat!"

"That," pronounced the veterinarian's daughter emphatically, "would make any beaver sick!"

Beaver was given an injection and some antibiotics and was soon eating and once again rearranging my house.

Schoolchildren learn more quickly:

Things I learned about beavers. When the young beavers build their lodges they are satisfied with their efforts. The chamber inside is then made. I don't mean to say that they wigt [sic] outside the lodge until it is completely finished but they build the bulk of the lodge first and then cut in from underneath to make the chamber.

Thank you for bringing the beaver. I learned a lot about them. They have oil to keep them waterproof, they have combs on there [sic] feet to combe [sic] the oil. I thought it funny when you told us about when your beaver put books in front of the stairways.

Love, Marie

Other children were not so precise:

Thank you for bringing the beaver. I liked the beaver. The best part I liked was when he squealed. I like animals too. I have one fish and two dogs.

> Yours truly, Richard.

Some children were impressed with other aspects:

I hope you come again. I liked beaver noses the best. I liked the webbed feet. Your show is great. It was funny when the beaver peed.

> Your friend, Pierre

Again, from Darren:

It does not matter about what the beaver did on the floor because that was what I liked best.

From Rick:

I loved the visit and "Beaver." It was funny when the beaver went to the washroom. Has "Beaver" ate any wooden chairs? I hope you drop by soon. I liked the way "Beaver" talks.

Letters from students are always encouraging. Also encouraging are letters from teachers:

Dear Audrey,

I want to thank you for coming to my class last Tuesday.

One little fellow, who has been very shy, very resistant to expressing himself, wrote in his science notebook:

"Today our class ikspeerienced [sic] the joy of TOW [sic] owls coming to visit . . ."! He said it so well! It is an encounter that for me reaffirms the place of us humans as caretakers in creation. You really communicate, by your words and who you are, that our job is to care for, to respect what God has created. Your visit will have a lasting effect on my students. I hope.

Thank you. Joy to you!

Sheila

The children learned. The adults? I have speculated about the conversation that likely took place in one family after a little boy met Quibble. His hand on the beaver's head, his dark eyes shining, he said: "My grandma is a trapper. I'm going to tell her she can't kill beavers any more."

PUBLIC APPEARANCES — TELEVISION AND MOVIES

The cameraman had us carefully posed so that the pond, the lodge, and the long, curving dam formed a suitable background for the interview about beavers. The program was to be lighthearted, entertaining.

"Beavers," the pretty young hostess began her questions gaily, "are the symbol of Canada. Why were they chosen for this honor?"

My answer was supposed to be as lighthearted and gay. It was supposed to flatter Canadians by saying we were as clever and industrious as beavers. Instead, I told the truth. "The beaver was chosen because the exploration and mapping of Canada was stimulated by the lust for beaver skins. Europeans and nations alike pushed farther and farther into the hinterlands killing beavers for the price of their hides. That is why the early explorers penetrated our country. Millions of beavers paid with their lives."

The camera clicked off. The interviewer was nonplussed. She tried again. "Couldn't you say the beaver was chosen because it works so hard?"

I'm a little stubborn about beavers. "No. Because what I said is the truth."

Probably that particular clip was never part of the final program. However, what I maintained is true: the beaver appears on our national symbols because of its economic importance, because, for money, we slaughtered millions and millions of them. We still kill beavers.

When they have made their public appearances, the beavers themselves have been much more entertaining than I. Beavers have enough personality and charm to become popular television stars. But they also have too much common sense. Though Quibble appeared in television segments and documentaries all around the world, he was unconscious of any need to flatter even his most distinguished hosts. He seemed to accept people as merely people; he was a beaver and no amount of fame or flattery would ever change that.

At present, with spinning satellites and the proliferation of computers and the Internet and web sites and all sorts of incomprehensible wonders, television is becoming mundane. Time was, and not that long ago, when television was the wonder. I can remember when radio was supreme. (Somehow I do not think the squeaks and grunts of a beaver would capture much of a radio audience!) Quibble did not comprehend any of it. Primitive, I suppose, but peaceful.

Though my first beaver, Swampy, never did reach the heights of fame that Quibble managed to achieve, he was the first of our animals to make such a public debut. Even at his first television special, he slept. He left it to me to be nervous on his second appearance.

Swampy's fame spread nonetheless. Actually, I would like to think the demand for television appearances grew due to his exceptionally sparkling personality. However, since beavers do not sparkle, the demand most likely arose from the fact that beavers that can be handled are relatively rare.

The cameras from Global Television came to the Sanctuary. The program was *That's Life*, with Peter Feniak. It was wintertime. Had Swampy been living in the wild, he would have been snug in his lodge, swimming freely under the ice only when he was hungry enough to eat the aspen sticks he had stored. But he lived with me. And because he needed more space and more aspen than my house could offer, he had been moved to the barn for the winter. He had built himself a large hay house under the goat's manger, where he was sleeping the winter away, emerging for his food or to sit with me and chat awhile, since no other beavers were available. (I think beavers are insatiable gossips.) In fairly authentic beaver fashion, his sleeping chamber was reached through a small tunnel, quite inaccessible to anyone but himself. I had warned him that he was scheduled to make a television appearance, but he merely grunted and trundled down his tunnel.

That winter, the goats lived downstairs in the barn with Danny, the horse. The skunks had their pen. A couple of raccoons ran free, one named Ben. I had not raised Ben. His owners, in Toronto, had decided late in November that he was no longer fit for an apartment. When the first snows of winter whirled, they brought Ben to me to set free. At that time of year freedom would have been certain death; thus, Ben lived in the barn.

The time for Swampy's television interview came. I preceded several television cameramen with clattering cameras and lights down the dark and narrow stairs. To Swampy and the other assorted animals it must have seemed cataclysmic! His tail switching back and forth, Ben crouched on a box, head low, back end up. He was afraid. He was angry. And he was about to attack! I grabbed him just before he tried to launch himself at a cameraman; there was not much time to do anything else.

Mr. Feniak spent the next half hour bandaging teeth and claw marks on my arms; the bite on the back of my head did not show. The crew met the challenge of photographing a perfectly "unattacked" person by using angles at which bandages did not show.

But they had come to film Swampy. So I got down on my knees by the hay tunnel.

"Swampy," I called down his tunnel. "It's time! Come out!"

No movement.

"Swampy! Come!" (Beavers cannot be obedience trained.)

Nothing.

The crew stood waiting. Cameras were pointed at the tunnel opening. The lights glared.

"Beaver!"

We waited.

"Swampy. I'll give you a banana." Bribery often works with dogs. And raccoons. Nothing.

"Beaver. We're waiting."

Suddenly, movement. Brief scrambling, shuffling. Swampy emerged, blinked at the camera, sat up, scrubbed his face, grunted, turned and waddled back down the tunnel. The crew had to be satisfied with that.

Switchback was a children's program televised in an Ottawa studio, and the director of the series wanted a live beaver very badly. I was not particularly co-operative; Ottawa is a five-hour drive from Rosseau. The program was scheduled for ten o'clock in the morning, and because it was winter, driving would be unpredictable.

The director offered to pay airfare. Apart from the fact that catching an airplane would mean a drive to either North Bay (two-and-a-half hours) or Toronto (three-and-a-half hours), flying would also mean that Quib would have to travel in a cage in the hold of an airplane. That stress would have been unbearable for both of us. Next, they offered me a hotel room in Ottawa and a taxi to the studio. I stipulated that Quibble would have to be permitted to stay in the hotel room with me. Perhaps visualizing a beaver in a cage, they agreed. I didn't tell them that Quib would be quite free to roam the entire room if he cared to.

So we set off for Ottawa, the sun shining, music on the radio, Quib roaming freely in the back of the station wagon. Highway 60 seemed almost deserted. We made good time all the way to Algonquin Park, through the park and out the eastern gate.

No traffic, easy driving, police siren.

Yes, I was breaking the speed limit. No, I had not actually realized it. Of course, I understood that ignorance was no excuse. Meekly, I took the ticket. Sixty dollars. And then the policeman saw Quibble observing the whole proceeding from the back.

The policeman was intrigued. "Is that a beaver?"

Inward thought: "No, it's a bull moose."

Outwardly, "Yes, sir."

"Why do you have a beaver?"

I explained.

"Interesting," he said, stroking his chin and stepping back from the car. We drove slowly away. Could he, on meditation, produce a remote law forbidding beavers in the back seats of station wagons?

Once in Ottawa, where I expected to be utterly confused because the city is considerably bigger than Rosseau, we found the Plaza Hotel relatively quickly. We parked in the underground garage. I coaxed Quibble into his travelling cage, found the elevator, ignored all raised eyebrows and proceeded to the room reserved for us.

Room? We were guests of CBC Television. We had a suite! Quibble, free again, ponderously explored the kitchenette, the bathroom and the sitting room/bedroom. Carefully, he investigated the sofa, the long curtains, the bathtub. Finally, he declared that the best place to sleep was on the soft rug under the sink.

Because I still would not leave Quib alone, our meals arrived by room service. The bellboy stared at the sleeping animal. "Is that a beaver?" (A polite answer to that question will have to be devised.) "What's he doing here?"

I told him.

"Gosh, I've seen dogs here and cats. Once a rabbit . . . Can I bring the other guys up?"

That evening a good number of visitors came to see Quib. He showed no territorial tendency, he simply ignored everyone. Only once did he even comment. He was sitting by the floor-length windows, thinking — who knows? Suddenly he turned and pulled the curtains aside. Our room in the hotel was quite high. Below us, in darkness, spread the lights of Ottawa.

Ottawa, capital of the country that holds the beaver as its symbol.

Quib looked for a long, long moment, said, "Humph!" dropped the curtain, then walked away.

Perhaps it was merely a comment on the Mulroney government.

All night the snow fell. In the morning travel was slippery. The taxi driver, regarding the cage, frowned a little. "Is that a beaver?"

There must be an answer.

"He'd better go in the trunk."

"No. On my knee, or we get another taxi."

By the time we arrived at the studio, Quib had managed to charm the driver so much that he volunteered to wait until the program was over to take us back to the hotel.

The studio was surprisingly small. I had to submit to the application of some makeup; Quib was handsome enough without it. We were moved into position during a commercial. The audience of children was walled away from us by a bank of cameras. The host (whose name I never did know) seemed something of a clown. Whoever had written the questions the children asked was more interested in laughs than in information; however, I managed to deliver one anti-trapping line before the incredibly short segment was over. I could not believe that so much money had been been spent for so short an appearance.

Our taxi driver was waiting to take us back to the hotel.

Something about television — watching it — interested Quibble. I know that to say he was interested in politics would be anthropomorphic, but I do remember one comment he had to make.

Readers may remember the night Joe Clark, briefly prime minister of Canada, was undergoing a leadership review. Quibby was squatting in front of the television set and, whatever his motives, was watching. When Mr. Clark finally made the announcement that he was going to step down, Quibby sat quiet (considering?) for a moment, said, "Humph!" waddled away and did not watch television for the remainder of the evening. This comment being a repeat of what he had said about Prime Minister Mulroney's Ottawa. I concluded that he was not a Conservative! Further than that, I will not comment.

One young woman came all the way from China to host a TV program to be shown in her homeland. She was one of the most beautiful women I have ever seen. Dressed exquisitely, she would have fit in perfectly in the salons of Paris or Rome. Unfortunately, she came to Muskoka in the early spring — mud season. Only beavers truly love mud!

Because her cameraman wanted the interview with Quibble to take place beside his pond, where he had been spending his days piling mud and arranging sticks, twigs and stones of all shapes and sizes, she would have to contend with mud. Quibble, of course, was somewhat muddy himself. However, he received her with, for him, maximum passivity. He did not clasp her legs or lovely skirt in his muddy paws or drag her out of his enclosure; he decided to ignore her. He continued solemnly with his work. Perhaps it is my imagination that the only time he paused, sat up and stared at her was when she asked her first question: "How do you obedience train a beaver?"

The host of a European television program was also quite beautiful. But this time I was more incensed and angry than Quib was. She had the supreme lack of sensitivity to arrive wearing a beaver fur coat! Apparently the theme of the program was to be the fur trade in Canada. The crew had travelled from Quebec to the Northwest Territories, interviewing trappers and photographing dead beavers, but they had not been able to find a live beaver for their program. And so, having heard of Quibble, they phoned the Sanctuary.

"Could we film your beaver?"

I was not friendly. "For a documentary on the fur trade?"

He said, "We haven't been able to find a live beaver."

I answered, "Not if you film people who kill them."

There was a long pause. "I take it you don't like the fur trade?" European charm began to creep into his voice. He continued, so very charming, "Perhaps you could state your opinion and reason for it."

That I could do!

All might have gone well if the host had not arrived wearing a coat made of dead beavers — killed for human fashion. If Quibble recognized it, he never said a word. I recognized it and said a good many. I expect they were all edited out of the program. By this time I think I was achieving some competence in being edited out!

I did not find television appearances, even as second string to a beaver, very easy. But I do understand that the media has immense power with the public. And I will do anything to help the public understand the wonder of creatures, especially beavers.

Humans who kill for a living find it necessary to justify their actions. Conscience? How many thousands upon thousands of people heard, as I did one day on the CBC, about a woman who had built a very lucrative business cutting beaver hides into very narrow strips and then knitting them or weaving them into unique garments that are carried by the high-fashion industry. She explained that trapping and killing wild things, especially beavers, is not only easily justified but actually contributes to their welfare. After all, if the animal dies in a trap, it will not die of starvation, accident or disease. True enough. Still, perhaps the beaver might prefer to live a long, interesting life until it dies in as natural a way as a human might do, of old age.

Again on the CBC, I heard a trapper from the Dorset area interviewed. He said, "When I see I have caught a healthy beaver, I have to remember he might have been killed by some predator or he might breed too many beavers and then they wouldn't have anything to eat and die of starvation." Interesting justification! Such nonsense. I cannot in all conscience allow such attitudes to go unchallenged. I wish the whole world could know how splendid beavers are!

Grey Owl is the man most often associated with beavers. In my long-ago youth he was regarded as a great hero. Then along came the debunkers who revealed that he was not actually an Indian, had several wives, and was from time to time too attached to the bottle. None of which in any way changed all the good things he did for beavers.

More recently, people have begun to realize that in many ways Grey Owl was a great man. So they now make movies about him. In 1998, a Hollywood studio made a movie in Quebec. One of their most handsome, expensive actors, who had played many roles in movies as a spy, was playing the lead as Grey Owl. Perhaps the real Grey Owl might have been flattered, but he would almost certainly have been amused at the effort. Hollywood had almost all it needed for a good movie: great star, cameras, extras, all sorts of equipment, and money. But no beavers.

Then in March, the phone rang at the Sanctuary. A cultured voice at the other end of the line explained the greatness of the movie to be produced, then asked, "Do you by any chance have beaver kits we could use?"

"No," I replied. "They are not even born until May or June."

"But, we need one now!"

Sorry Hollywood, God arranged the seasons, we didn't. And I was pretty sure the beavers themselves would not change their schedule even to accommodate the "super spy" who was playing the role of Grey Owl. I love it when the beavers have the last word!

Hollywood managed to find a beaver kit somewhere much farther south, in the United States, where Hollywood is held in much higher esteem — except by beavers. The kit and his handler arrived in Quebec, where the movie about the saviour of the beavers was under production — with a single beaver kit. He had to play several roles, but since beavers resemble each other closely, the duplication was no great problem. For a while the kit was submissive, allowing himself to be handled, posed, confined and cuddled. And then one day, when all the attention was focused on the star himself, the little beaver simply slipped into the water and swam away.

Hollywood hunted, but they never found him. The movie had to be finished with a fake beaver. I hope that somewhere, in a quiet lake in Quebec, a little beaver who turned his back on fame and fortune is quietly nibbling on lily pads and bulrush roots.

Quib was scheduled to star in a Grey Owl movie produced by the BBC. The television star and crew came all the way from England. This program was to be as accurate a documentary as possible and to begin with black-and-white footage of the actual Archie Belaney with his own real beavers — a very good beginning. Full color would be used to feature Quibble, teaching us about real beavers. Ojibway friends came down from the Shawinigan First Nation Reserve to act in the opening scenes. High up on a rocky point of land at the Sanctuary, they built a bonfire. With a million stars overhead, the firelight flickered on the weathered face of a Native elder and the intent faces of listening children. The elder told stories of the beavers at the beginning of all things, when the beaver helped the Creator form the great continent on which we live. He told of the long and honorable association between people and beavers before the advent of the fur trade, long, long ago.

By this stage of his life, Quib had taken over the entire basement of my house. The basement has the potential to be quite lovely. The walls are old fieldstone built one hundred years ago. At one end, quite unplanned and evidently beyond remedy (especially at spring thaw or after a heavy rain), there is a little flowing stream. I supplied straw to substitute for mud and lots of sticks, so that Quib could build a fairly presentable lodge under the cellar stairs. Like most beaver lodges, little short of dynamite could destroy it. Of course, I had no intentions of destroying it.

As with Swampy in the barn, all the BBC crew, with cameras and lights, clambered down the basement stairs immediately over Quib's head. When all was ready, with lights and cameras trained on the lodge entrance, I called Quib.

No answer.

"Quib?"

After a while, we heard a somewhat sulky grunt, a movement, then Quib emerged. Having learned from our experience with Swampy, I caught him quickly and sat him on my knee. He allowed me to show the children of Britain all the beaver specialties: his long, orange teeth; his little ears; his little front feet and his huge, webbed back feet. And, of course, his tail.

Afterward, grumbling mightily, Quib disappeared into his lodge. Like an eccentric celebrity, he declared the interview over!

Beavers and Human Predators

5

CHINOOK AND TATTERTAIL

Chinook was raised by two of our Sanctuary foster parents, Marvin and Merilan Barnes. They had fostered dozens of raccoons and squirrels, rabbits and birds, and then they received a call about an orphaned beaver. Merilan has written the following account of Chinook's early days, when he was one of their charges.

> Aspen Valley Wildlife Sanctuary is the main center of a group of people who look after injured and orphaned wildlife. This center has many arms reaching out from it. These arms are the private homes of volunteers who look after injured and orphaned animals. We are one of those arms, and that is how we became a part of this beaver's life.
>
> On June 15, 1998, our phone rang, and a very kind and concerned cottager on Gull Lake asked for help. She explained that she had a baby beaver that had been swimming frantically for about thirty-six hours with no adult beaver in sight.
>
> Our first concern was the beaver. We would find out all the details later. We got directions and within thirty minutes of the call were at the pick-up site.

Chinook, very small for his age and not recovered completely from his burns. His coat was very sparse.

She handed me a towel with something small and lightweight inside. Quickly, I asked for some background details on why this beaver was alone. She explained that another cottager on the lake had dynamited a beaver house, killing all but this one. Thanking her for her concern, we quickly headed for home to attend to our new charge.

On our trip home I slowly opened its towel and came face to face with a beaver no bigger than a small, newborn puppy. The little eyes looking up at me were filled with fear and exhaustion. We stared at each other, and I could sense the plea for help and understanding coming from this wee bundle.

Now June, the Sanctuary was well into its busiest time, with many babies of all kinds on hand and many more coming in daily. There was no one with lots of spare time just to attend to this wee beaver. We had to make a decision to keep her or send her to people who were already overloaded with responsibility. We decided to keep her and try our best to do the right things.

On close inspection we found burns from the blast on all four feet. These burns had to be tended to right away. Using natural remedies, we applied juice of an aloe stem very carefully to each burn on the feet and between the toes.

Next it was time to try to get some formula into this wee one. We prepared a formula that is just for vegetarians. We tried a small baby's bottle, but this beaver would have no part of it. She had to be fed, though, so we used an eyedropper and were able to get a bit into her. On seeing what little amount she took, we knew that feeding time was going to have to be frequent. We set up a schedule of feeding every hour on the hour until the intake could be increased.

We made a warm bed in a small box, with a soft blanket and hot-water bottle under the blanket. Now I know that June is a warm month, but this little one needed extra warmth due to the trauma and shock that she was going through. Our vigil had begun, and by rotating turns we were able to take full care of the beaver plus look after the other baby animals in our care.

A very close vigil was kept on our new baby, and on the third day we noticed that her bowels started working overtime. A constant flow of brown liquid came from her rectum and a small amount of clear liquid dribbled out of her mouth. Within hours our fat bundle became bones with a fur covering, and such sad eyes.

"Dear God," we were losing her. Now it was time for us to panic and pray. The feeding continued with the eyedropper, plus a dose of Strawberry Extract to counteract the diarrhea. The diarrhea stopped, but the beaver was not regaining weight, even with the increased formula intake.

Again, we put our heads together and prayed. We decided to add pureed yams and green beans to the formula. The nutrients in yams are similar to the bulb of a water lily, a natural beaver food. The green beans were in place of green leaves.

During this time we were the only ones around the beaver, except for our Boxer dog, who liked to wash the beaver's face. Next, it was time to introduce our granddaughter and grandson.

Whether it was because they were young I do not know, but the beaver just loved them. It crawled all over them and played, and when it got tired it curled up on our granddaughter's knee and went to sleep.

Because it is difficult to know the sex of a beaver, we had not given it a name. The job was given to our grandchildren, who named it Baby Bee Jade, as they felt it was a girl. Baby Bee did not like to be alone, and many nights she slept soundly beside me and during the day was carried around from room to room as we worked.

We decided that to build up the strength in her legs we should carry her less and let her follow us on her own. This she did with great pleasure until we got out of her sight. When that happened she would sit and make crying sounds until we backtracked so she could see us. She would then continue to follow, grumbling all the time. She missed being carried.

As Bee gradually got stronger and started to like being in the water, we bought a child's swimming pool. We set this up on our front lawn, and four times a day we walked out to the pool, with Bee right behind us. In she would go, and she would swim around, dive, then get up on a flat rock that was placed in the center of the pool. We noticed that it took a long time for Bee to dry off, and found out much later that her oil glands were not working right, a condition caused by the trauma she suffered from the blast. Her little feet were slowly healing, but the skin was very dry, so we started gently rubbing mineral oil on them to try to moisten the skin.

Despite her interest in the pool, Baby Bee was not one for the outdoors. We would take her out onto the lawn, trying to get her to walk around and maybe nibble on some leaves or grass. But this was not what Bee wanted. She would head straight for the house with no stops along the way. No matter how far we would take her out into the yard, she would follow our trail back to the house. It was funny watching this little thing, with her distinctive wiggle, go across the lawn, determined to get where she wanted to be.

We gradually began to introduce solids: aspen leaves and small branches, a bit of romaine lettuce and some apples, cut-up yams, blueberries, broccoli, raspberry leaves and a bit of white potato. All of this was given to her fresh daily along with her formula, which was now being given by syringe. With this combination, she gained weight rapidly. Another battle won.

Baby Bee liked to play and for some reason decided that the male part of our team was her playmate. She would sit on her behind and rise up and take her front paws and box with my husband. He, in turn, would gently pat her back, and the boxing match was on.

When she tired of this, she would come to me to snuggle on my chest with her head under her chin. It was time for me to pet her and scratch behind her ears and just give her some loving.

She gave us many hours of entertainment, dragging her blanket from one spot to another, changing the area where her bed was. If we took it back to the original place, she would go get it and take it where she wanted it, while making a vocal protest. Sometimes she would steal my slipper, put it where she wanted it, then climb into it and have a quick nap. She also liked to play tug-of-war with the slipper, and when we let her win she would proudly walk away with the slipper in her mouth.

One day, we were surprised with a gift of a baby Pomeranian puppy about the size of Baby Bee. We introduced them and it was love at first sight. They played together, ate together and slept together. Bee did not want our attention so much now, and we missed that, but she was growing and becoming more independent, which was good. She still came for her boxing matches and attention, but not as often. The tug-of-war game was now played with the pup.

Little Bee's food intake was increasing greatly, and she was now piling her aspen branches up in the style of a beaver house. We continued to apply mineral oil to her feet and legs, as they were still dry and scaly.

We watched her grow and knew the time to move her was drawing near. She needed a bigger place, a place where she could have more aspen branches and an indoor pool for the winter, and a place with straw for bedding. We did not have all of this, but the Sanctuary did.

Less time was required for her care, as she played, ate and slept when she wanted. She was no longer on her formula, just solids, and was drinking water on her own. We kept her for an extra week so that we could enjoy her and build up more memories.

It was now October, and Bee needed to be in her new home so she could get settled down for the winter. We took the Pomeranian puppy with her for company on the ride up. With tears in our hearts, we turned Baby Bee Jade over to Audrey at the Sanctuary.

After a short time with Audrey, it was decided that Baby Bee was a boy, and he was renamed Chinook. We go to see him as often as possible, and he remembers us. In our hearts and minds, he will always be our Baby Bee Jade, and we will always remember and love him.

Chinook spent the winter in a special new enclosure downstairs in the house. He had a kennel, a bathtub for swimming, lots of straw, and yams, apples, carrots and romaine lettuce. He ate. He grew. He was friendly, chatty. All that seemed strange about him (but likely somehow connected to the explosion that orphaned him) was that he did not really like water. He would drink it but not swim in it — the only beaver I had ever known who did not like to be wet! His second problem, quite obviously a result of the explosion, was that if he heard any sudden or loud sound, he would panic. In the room directly above his enclosure stood my piano, but his fear was so evident that, for the winter he was inside, I had to stop playing it. And I had to ignore my friends who unkindly suggested that his objection to my playing was not a fear of noise, but almost certainly a matter of musical taste.

Spring came, and the construction of a large new beaver enclosure was begun. The excavator scooped great chunks of earth; the flowing spring from the hillside turned into a stream and the new pond filled and flowed through. An acre of ground surrounding the pond was fenced off, the fence several feet underground as well as six feet above. New grass grew green and tall. We supplied aspen. We wanted Chinook to learn to be a real beaver — a beaver who liked water!

After he was moved into the enclosure, his fear of water took a day or so to overcome. Twice he accidentally slid down a muddy bank and landed in the pond. Panic! With much scrambling and tail smacking, he was soon out of the water, shaking and grooming himself frantically. He slept in the dry straw in a small A-frame, on dry land. He could not be coaxed into the water. To make a loud noise behind him so that he would jump in seemed too cruel. Then, some revelation must have taken place at night, for one morning we found him swimming peacefully and placidly, completely natural and obviously happy.

I rather wished that I could take my piano outside and test for any improvement in his musical appreciation.

The fact that beavers do not read biology books is just fine; beavers do not waste much time! Chinook did not know he would not be welcomed by a family of beavers not his own. For a few weeks he was quite content, then one night he found a very small hole in the fence. A violent rainstorm had washed the mud out of a place where a fencing joint was not quite secure. So, in the dark, Chinook wandered out, up the lane and down the hill to the pond where the pond beavers live. For the first time since he had lost his own family, he encountered other beavers.

No one was there to witness the actual meeting, but in the morning I saw him swimming with them. He ate with them and he was in the lodge. For several days this seemed to be a very happy arrangement and seemed to solve a problem for us. However, though Chinook had not read biology books, I had, and I knew that it could be very difficult to persuade two unrelated beavers to share a pond.

Meanwhile the Sanctuary had given haven to an older beaver who had come from Toronto. She had been spattered with buckshot. We gave her the name Tattertail.

The Tattertail story began, as so many stories do, with a phone call. This call was from the Wildlife Department of the Toronto Humane Society. "We have a beaver," Paloma said. "It's pretty sick. What should we do?"

Though she was not exactly asking me to take the beaver, she is a good friend and knows me quite well, so she was not really surprised when I answered, "Why don't you send it up and let us care for it?"

She gave no argument.

Later that afternoon I met the Humane Society van halfway between the Sanctuary and Toronto, and the beaver came home. She was lethargic, thin, dull-coated, and big. Her tail was torn, missing several large chunks — a mess. Once here, we gave her warm, clean straw, a small pond of fresh water, aspen, yams, apples and antibiotics. At first we did not know the reason for her illness; then we did, and I wrote the following letter, which was printed in the *Toronto Star*.

Who shot gentle, old beaver full of buckshot? Toronto is a poorer place than it was a few days ago. I am aware of the surging human life in the city — and also of the quiet ravines where the rivers and woods still give homes to the wildlife, which is such an important part of our Canadian heritage. Some beavers live in those ravines going quietly about their lives, adapting to our intrusion.

Perhaps there are not many beavers left but they lived there long, long before any humans came, making the valleys green, providing ponds — building the foundations of our natural environment. We pay such homage to the beaver — the symbol of Canada, trademark for department stores and lumber companies. We glamourize Grey Owl as a national hero. Perhaps we should learn to understand and appreciate the real, living animal.

Early in May, the Toronto Humane Society (THS) was called down to the waterfront by Ontario Place. A beaver had washed ashore. She was badly injured. Full of buckshot.

The Aspen Valley Wildlife Sanctuary is a richer place now. Because I have been working with and caring for beavers for more than twenty-five years, the THS asked if we would help the beaver and we have had her in our care since May 4. She is very large and very old. She is a gentle, wise animal of immense dignity.

We call her Tattertail because of the condition of her tail. As we

114

work to drain the infection from the dozens of wounds, she submits quietly. We pray she will live.

To the human who shot the beaver, I hope you learn the importance of wildlife, even in the city, respect it, appreciate it and let it be. Failing that, I hope someone shoots your backside full of buckshot!

The letter brought a flurry of attention. Tattertail's story was covered in several newspapers, stimulated dozens of phone calls and earned an interview on the CBC. A great deal of support and under-standing emerged.

Tattertail was a very sick beaver when we received her at the Sanctuary. Pus oozed from the dozens of small wounds where the pellets had penetrated. Tony, our Sanctuary manager, along with Janet, his assistant, held the beaver, drained the pus, gave the needle with the antibiotic, and cleaned the wounds daily. At first the beaver did not resist. When resistance began, we celebrated. She was recovering! Tattertail's recovery was slow but steady.

Again, I was making the assumption that Tattertail was female. Certainly her lack of aggression was because of her physical condition, not necessarily because of her sex. Subsequent observations have, I think, confirmed that her instincts are strongly maternal. I also think she is a fairly old beaver, as beavers continue to grow all their lives, and she is very large. More than that, as she recovered I began to see in her eyes not only age, but wisdom.

It was while Tattertail was receiving intensive care in the barn that Chinook, now a yearling beaver, found the small escape hole in the fencing around the enclosure and wandered off to the larger pond where the pond beavers lived.

Since Tatterail was recovering nicely and the small enclosure with a pond was now empty, we decided that we could safely put her into the abandoned pond. Perhaps Chinook became aware that another beaver was in his former place and was not ready to relinquish all territorial claims, for one morning I found that he had deserted the pond beavers and was outside the fence of the enclosure, complaining, demanding to be let in. I opened the gate. Quickly, still complaining or explaining (I do not know which), he trundled in. He checked for yams, apples and romaine lettuce. He checked the water. He found Tattertail.

The conversation which took place is, of course, a matter of speculation; however, as time passed, some sort of friendship seemed to develop. I rather think that Tattertail had discovered a totally ignorant young beaver and felt it her responsibility to teach him what being a beaver really involved. He left his A-frame and began to live with her in a cave, its entrance tunnel under the water, in the bank. Then her teaching began.

Tattertail felt that a good diet was important for a beaver. Not only was Chinook to rely on the apples and yams that we supplied, but Tattertail also taught him to eat the bark from aspen branches and to graze on grass, dandelion, plantain and trefoil, on water-lily pads and roots.

After his food education, he had to learn construction, and dam construction came first. Tattertail taught Chinook to carry armloads of mud and sticks for this purpose. Even though the summer was hot and dry, their pond began to grow. Next was lodge construction with a roof-top ventilation hole. More mud and stick carrying. Tattertail kept Chinook busy.

For the remainder of the time Tattertail stayed with us at the Sanctuary, she and Chinook became a beaver family — eating together, working together, swimming together, and sleeping together. A strange but remarkable twosome!

That summer was a summer of long, hot drought. The water level in the pond went down and down. But Tattertail knew what to do. Where the pond narrowed to a very small stream, she began to build a dam. Both she and Chinook packed mud and sticks so compactly that the water level in their pond began to rise. The water in the duck pond, into which the small stream flowed, dried up. The ducks were quite perturbed. The beavers did not notice.

Once, during the construction, I went to the fence to watch. Chinook took the excuse to drop his armload of mud and waddle up the bank to see me. Tattertail dropped hers and was right behind him. He stopped, and if he had been human, he would have shrugged his shoulders. He turned, followed her back to the creek and resumed his work. Tattertail was a no-nonsense beaver!

Tattertail is, of course, unaware of the degree of fame the *Toronto Star* newspaper accorded her. On visiting days at the Sanctuary, people asked, "And where is that Tattertail?" The beavers were in an outdoor enclosure, and the ever-friendly Chinook would come to the fence and allow the visitors to admire him. But Tattertail stayed in the den she had hollowed out under the bank of the pond.

She did, however, make one brief appearance, the day of the CBC interview. The interviewer, Mary Wiens, and her children had come from Toronto. I had hoped that Tattertail would be co-operative, more co-operative than Quibble had been with the BBC crew that had crossed the Atlantic for the brief glimpse Quib allowed them. After Mary had gathered a great deal of beaver information, she asked, "And now, may I meet Tattertail?"

"I hope so," I said. No promises.

We went to the enclosure. We stood at the edge of the pond. Tentatively, I called, "Tattertail!"

The water rippled. A trail of bubbles, showing a beaver was just below the surface, swept in a circle and emerged at our feet. Chinook, of course. We admired him and waited again. And waited.

"Tattertail!"

Again the water quivered. Again, a trail of bubbles. Then the big beaver surfaced for just a moment. We saw how sleek and fat she had become. Then, with a thrust of her tattered tail she was beneath the surface again and back to her den. Beavers are not necessarily good at public relations!

Winter was coming. Both Tattertail and Chinook were as fat as bears about to hibernate; but beavers do not hibernate. Chinook had never spent a winter outside, so I had to discuss the situation with Tattertail. "You can do all the right beaver 'things' here," I informed her, as she totally ignored me, "or you can spend the winter in the barn."

However, she already had the matter well in hand, and Chinook worked along with her. I supplied aspen branches (actually at least two trees worth of aspen branches, as fortunately a neighbor up the road was clearing land and we were able to drag entire trees down to the beaver enclosure). The beavers worked. Beavers usually have a ventilation hole in their lodges, and these two built a dome over the hole in the roof of their cave. Then they covered the bankside with branches down to the underwater entrance. When I stood near the lodge, I could often hear the soft chatter of beavers inside.

The temperature dropped. Ice skimmed the pond. When I took the usual bag of apples, yams, carrots and corn cobs out to the A-frame, I saw no sign of activity.

"Chinook?" I called, realizing Tattertail was unlikely to respond.

"Chinook!" I saw a long, dark shape gliding under the ice, as silent and graceful as a dancer. Then, at my feet, a cracking of ice and a beaver head broke through — Chinook, looking for his dinner and jauntily wearing an icy cap. As the weather grew colder and the ice thicker, the beavers could not break the ice quite so casually, but all winter they maintained a piece of open water at the spot where the stream flowed into the enclosure. All winter I put apples, yams and carrots in the water there and so was able to supply food. Aspen branches, left on the ice near the hole, always disappeared.

Meanwhile, Tattertail did not know that we were capitalizing on her fame. We have an animal-oriented gift shop, open only on visiting

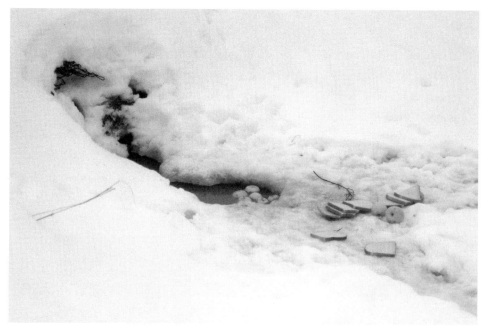

We fed Tattertail and Chinook through a hole in the ice all winter!

days. Money from this shop helps to pay the huge food bills of the Sanctuary. Many artists and craftspeople contribute their work, as did Tattertail. She ate bark from sticks, leaving them creamy clean, with chiselled teeth marks giving real distinction to the wood. Chinook most likely produced as many sticks as Tattertail did, but I signed each of them with Tattertail's name. They sold at twenty-five cents each. Many artists would envy Tattertail; her work has circled the globe.

After the two beavers had finished their construction, they had a well-built lodge where they were able to spend the winter. We continued to supply food, placing it near the entrance to the lodge in the late afternoon.

Then spring came. My journal entries for March indicate the developments:

SANCTUARY: MARCH 2000

MARCH 4: Four-thirty P.M. I have just come in from sitting beside the beaver pond. I put apples, yams and brown bread in the feed hole. I called Chinook. After a few moments I could hear him swishing around under the ice — first down by the lodge, and then near the small hole they have started around the ice, out from the lodge. He came to the big hole and swished around once so that I could see him, then went back under the ice. I could hear a good deal of activity under there, and looked up to see that Chinook was above water in the hole and watching me. I took a couple of pictures. He dove again, and I waited by the food hole and called again. Once more the water shook, and in a few moments the beaver came in, saw me and dove in. This time I caught a glimpse of the tail — Tattertail!

MARCH 6: A wonderfully warm, sunny afternoon. At about two o'clock I took apples and yams and a big aspen branch out to the food hole in the beaver pond. I had not seen either beaver for a day, although Chinook answered when I called yesterday. Today he came out onto the ice several times, huffing at me most mightily. I could hear him swimming under the ice. He surfaced at a melted spot just outside the lodge. I heard him swim across to the cave on the other side. Then he was out again. He came to my fingers but did not want to be patted. I suspect he wanted more food. I went to the house and came back with a corn cob; however, he did not come out again. I wonder if the fact that the coyotes were on the other side of the fence was what made him so huffy.

MARCH 8: Another wonderfully warm day and very muddy. A professional photographer was here taking pictures. Chinook came out but was quite huffy. He came to my fingertips but let me touch the top of his head only once. He seemed very leery of the photographer, and almost seemed to chase him out of the enclosure. Tattertail showed herself for just a moment.

MARCH 9: The photographer was here. Chinook came up on the bank, so we went into the enclosure to take pictures. Chinook was very huffy — he came to my fingers but did not really want to be touched. When we began to leave, Chinook followed us. I am not certain if he was chasing the photographer or just following.

MARCH 15: Yesterday I was in the beaver enclosure. Chinook came out of the water. I thought he wanted food, but actually he wanted me out of the enclosure. He took the apple I offered to him, but dropped it and began to chase me aggressively. I had to leave. I think he is quite capable now of going free. He is huge and aggressive and seems to be digging up grass roots on his own, and certainly cleaning up all the aspen we put into the enclosure.

The weather has been relatively warm, and the ice on the water is melting. Some places it still holds Chinook's weight, but he has trouble getting up onto the ice from the water because the edges keep breaking away.

MARCH 21: Chinook's pond is still mostly frozen except around the edges. The spade which he stole through his hole back in February has made its appearance, the handle standing through the ice. But today it was tossed on top of the lodge as though he was returning it because he did not need it anymore.

MARCH 23: A beautiful warm day. I took a couple of yams and went out to sit on the log beside the beaver pond to wait for Chinook. Tatterail appeared and did not seem disturbed that I was there. Then Chinook came out. They started to play. He rode on her tail and partway down her back. She rolled, they wrestled and had a wonderful time. Spring!

As the hole in the ice grew larger, I saw Chinook often, Tattertail occasionally. Chinook showed no tendency towards any renewal of friendship; the time had come for him to be free. We had a couple of alternatives: they both could go out to Quetico's pond (Quetico and whatever family he had acquired over the years had abandoned one lodge and moved further upstream, so an empty house was available there). Alternatively, we had begun to suspect our pond beavers had also moved farther up their particular stream and deserted their lodge under the dead tamarack. If we released Chinook and Tattertail into that pond, we would have to continue to supply food — aspen, yams and apples — because reasonably the pond beavers had likely moved only after having diminished the natural food supply at the pond.

Tattertail was completely wild. Chinook was maturing. Sometimes he would, somewhat tentatively, allow me to touch his head, rub his ears. Usually, he either totally ignored me or, huffing, would run at me to chase me out of the enclosure. Tattertail had been teaching him well the necessities of survival in the wild.

A television cameraman wanted footage of a beaver. Chinook would not make an appearance; he would not produce even a ripple on the water. Had the cameraman not, on previous occasions, viewed beavers in the same enclosure, he might have doubted my assertion that two large beavers lived in the lodge.

When another photographer, also interested in beaver pictures, came into the enclosure, he was slightly more fortunate. Momentarily, Chinook welcomed me, then he spotted the other intruder. He huffed, he put his head low, he charged.

True to her word, Merilan had not forgotten Chinook. Over the telephone, I tried to explain. "He is two years old now," I said. "In the wild, he would likely be leaving home."

"I still want to see him before he goes," she insisted.

"When you come," I warned Merilan and Marvin, acting as though I were some sort of authority on beavers (no one is, except perhaps another beaver), "don't be disappointed if he doesn't come when you call."

"I know," she said. "I won't. I just want to see him."

Merilan phoned again. "Marvin and I are coming up. We just want to visit him before he goes".

Naturally. Still, I was apprehensive. But they came. I was working up at the barn, and although I saw their van coming up the driveway, I could not go down immediately. Marvin was already in the enclosure when I got there. He was stooped down, Chinook at his feet, both of them deep in conversation. Merilan went in, and Chinook welcomed her, arms upstretched, grunting. I stayed outside the enclosure, watching a maturing beaver, separated from his people for more than a year, recognizing them, welcoming them, talking to them.

Chinook suddenly grunted softly, turned, trundled down the bank and slipped under the water into his lodge. For a few moments the water was quiet. Marvin and Merilan stood back. Then the water quaked, and Chinook reappeared.

In his mouth was a peeled stick, maybe a foot long and a few inches around. He trundled up the bank purposefully and came directly to Merilan. He stood up and carefully laid the stick on her feet, whimpered softly, turned, and silently returned to his lodge. This was his parting gift to her.

Chinook did not appear again.

A few days later we moved Tattertail and Chinook down to our small beaver lake. They took over the lodge, repairing the dam so that the water rose to a decent level. After that they perhaps decided that the food supply was not adequate for growing, hungry beavers, and they, too, moved upstream.

We are grateful that Tattertail, in serious condition when she arrived at the Sanctuary, recovered so well that she was able to lead Chinook to absolute freedom.

CODY'S STORY

I am writing this book for Cody because I promised her that I would. I promised her as I held her in my arms and knew that she was dying.

I cannot know each detail of the beginning of her story in anything more than the generalities that form the lives of most beavers. She would have been part of a family — a father, a mother, yearling brothers and sisters, siblings her own age. Though it's easiest for us to deny that beavers hold any affection for each other, my observations of many beavers have indicated very clearly that beavers are capable of deep affection that can last over many years.

Cody would have been born in May or June, nurtured with her siblings by her mother, given attention and care and teaching by both parents and yearlings, growing, learning, living quietly in some wetland of the northern woods. By the time it was necessary to gather the branches to be anchored near the lodge for winter food, Cody would have been old enough to help. As snow and cold came and the water froze over, the beavers lived in the warmth of their lodge, swimming out beneath the ice to eat the stored food.

That is where the trap was set.

I do not oppose trapping because of what I have been told or have read about its cruelty. Rather, I have walked traplines; I have seen torture and death.

I well remember one November when the world was beautiful, dusted lightly with snow. A trail leads off one end of our road for a mile, through tall woods to a small wilderness lake with a rocky island in the middle. I knew the water would be dark, the rocks and trees silvered, so I took my camera and two of the dogs to hike the short trail back to the lake. Kate was a black Labrador who understood life and the responsibilities that came with it. Duncan was a Labrador pup who did not take anything seriously.

The walk into the lake was lovely but uneventful. The adventure began on our return trip. Duncan, learning to walk in the woods without a leash, dutifully followed Kate — most of the time. On this day he ranged off, and I heard a scramble as he plunged down into the ravine. Kate cocked her head and followed him. I called them both but was totally ignored. I called again, but even obedient Kate failed to return. So I, too, followed.

When I looked down into the ravine I saw both dogs, noses up, investigating a most peculiar bundle tied several feet up a tree. Puzzled, I went down.

A bundle of skinned muskrats and a baby beaver hung by their tails — bait for a trap. The little beaver's eyes were open: the same beaver's eyes that would once have shone so splendidly with light as he played on the water. But these eyes were dull with death. A log was propped up near the bundle, and on it a leg-hold trap, sprung, with a torn raccoon body dangling from it. The woods around me were no longer beautiful. I untwisted the wire anchoring the trap and took it with me. It had killed its last raccoon.

Now the dogs followed obediently. Carrying (stealing) the trap, I tried not to think of the skinned muskrat and the beaver and the rotting raccoon. A raven rose out of the ravine, and once again, the dogs disappeared. This time I followed immediately.

Again, bait at the end of a leaning log, a skinned beaver hanging by its tail. The raven had already feasted on the beaver, so it had no eyes.

But the trap was still not sprung. I released the beaver and buried it gently under the fallen leaves. Then I removed the trap and carried it home as well.

I was angry and not thinking clearly. On the porch I began to examine the trap more closely. It sprang closed. My fingers were caught tight in its steel grip. I did not cry out. For a long moment my entire arm was numb, then the pain began — intense, throbbing pain.

I thought, "This would not kill an animal. They would live a long time. And they could know this pain until they died." I could not budge the jaws of that trap. My fingers throbbed and swelled. And I was alone.

Well, when there is no help, one must help oneself. I sat on the porch step and tried to figure out how to release the trap, thinking, "I've got to hurry. My fingers are crushed," and telling myself, "This is how those little beavers likely died, and dying would take hours." Finally, and I still don't know what piece of the mechanism I touched, I moved something that opened the jaws just enough for me to inch my fingers out. The swelling and bruising lasted for days.

I cannot tell you exactly how Cody was caught in such a trap. But I can share with you a true story written by a friend. The trapper about whom he talks was a leading resident of our village and a respected warden of the church.

When I was thirteen years old, I was excited with my opportunity to help a local trapper tend his lines. The first week we snow-shoed to the beaver floods and set a number of traps. They were leg-hold traps that were set near the shore where the beaver entered the water through a hole in the ice. The traps were also attached to a wire doubly anchored, one end at the shore, the other in deeper water. The object was to cause the animal to step into the trap and then slide down the one-way wire until the water was deep enough to drown it.

The second week, we checked those traps that had been set one week earlier. One small beaver was caught in the first trap. We eventually found another, but this one was not yet dead. This beaver was large and had caught his hind foot in the trap instead of the preferred front foot. As a result he had not drowned in the deeper water. With time, plenty of time, he had freed the anchor in the deep water and had clawed and struggled so hard and so long that the shore-line anchor now appeared to be a good eight to ten feet out into the water, because the beaver had actually clawed the bank away. His hind leg was in tatters and his front paws were worn to the bone. The trapper clubbed the beaver over the head to stun him and then held his head under the water until he drowned. I remember well the desperate beaver's last attempt at escape as his legs splashed everywhere in an effort to gain one final breath. It was the trapper's guess that the beaver had been in the trap for four to five days.

Cody's life began some distance from here. Somehow, she tore her back feet out of such a trap, heaved herself up on the ice, and, in complete panic, began to run. From this point, her story can be accurately documented.

The temperature those nights was about minus twenty-five degrees Fahrenheit (-32C). Cody was found huddled under some alders, far out in the bush along a snowmobile trail. The compassionate people who picked her up wrapped her in an extra jacket and took her to the nearest veterinarian. The veterinarian, after giving her the help he could, drove three hundred miles to bring her to the Sanctuary.

The beaver lay quietly on my knee, wrapped in a towel. Docile. Too docile.

"I could not find anything wrong," said the veterinarian. "A bit of an injury to one foot — maybe a touch of frostbite." Not many veterinarians are asked to diagnose a wild beaver in the middle of winter. "She's been eating," he added, "but she's not moving much."

That veterinarian had made the long, long trip because he cared. We all cared, standing there, sitting there, watching the quiet young beaver — too quiet.

Still, another beaver! We had wanted a companion for Chinook, who was spending the first winter of his life alone in the warm, hay-filled enclosure downstairs in the house. Beavers are family creatures, so perhaps Cody could be his friend. Tony built a second enclosure that shared one wall with Chinook's. When they had accepted each other, we would remove the wall and the two beavers could be together. Having a pair would make release time so much more plausible, too.

So, Cody arrived, quiet, apprehensive, and gentle. Too gentle. Something was not quite right.

First we made her a smaller enclosure, close to the warmth of the wood stove. Into this enclosure beside the stove, we put warm blankets. She seemed to snuggle into them as though even there, with the wood stove nearby, she could not get warm enough. I talked to her. She responded with soft, gentle grunts. I continued to let her swim in warm water in the bathtub.

She ate well — yams, bananas, apples, grapes, and kibble. But only when we took her for a swim in warmer water in the bathtub did she show evidence of being a wild-raised beaver: she would drum with her tail and attempt to dive, an attempt always thwarted because no bathtub is deep enough for a real beaver!

I estimated that she was about the same age as Chinook, and was so hopeful for their relationship. I think Chinook knew that another beaver was in the house just at the head of the stairs, and sometimes he grunted loudly and urgently. Perhaps he was hopeful, too. But Cody did not respond. Something was definitely wrong.

A few days passed when, one evening, I was sitting in the armchair, the fire warming the house. Cody was wrapped in a towel on my knee.

I could hear Chinook moving in the hay downstairs. "A few more days," I promised him, "and we will give you a friend." In my arms, Cody stirred. I thought she might want to go for a swim, so I ran warm water into the bathtub and eased her gently into it.

For the first time, I saw the skin was peeling from the bottom of her back feet. When she had finished her swim, I dried her feet carefully then put her back into her cage. The next morning, when Tony arrived at the Sanctuary, I told him about Cody's feet. Again, we uncovered her and looked.

"Bad frostbite," he said.

At that time we had no idea just how bad it would be. Again in the evening, when Cody was very quiet and content on my lap, I could not help watching her feet. The skin peeled away, leaving great, pulpy masses — first one foot and then the other. Then one toe broke away and lay in the towel. I thought, "Perhaps only one foot is that bad. Maybe we will have to amputate only one foot. She could still swim. Even if we have to keep her at the Sanctuary, she could still have a good life. . . ."

She lost more toes. A day later, the skin began to peel off her tail, leaving it pink and raw. I wondered where the trapper was. He no doubt cursed the trap that had not held the beaver.

And where was the lady who wanted a fine fur coat?

Cody's back feet began to fall off. We knew that all we could do for her was to give her a merciful death. As we drove to the veterinarian's office, the flesh began to fall away from her right arm.

As Cody went gently to sleep, I promised her that I would tell her story again and again and again until, some day, there would be no trappers and no equally guilty people in fine fur coats.

Chinook spent his first winter alone.

Twenty-First Century Beavers

6

BEAVERS OF THE NEW MILLENNIUM

January 2000

When, this January, a new century and a new millennium began, as the snow swirled around the house and the fire burned brightly in the wood stove, there was time to contemplate the arrival of the beavers who are with us now at the Sanctuary.

Out in two large stalls in the barn live two pairs of magnificent beavers — huge, coats glistening with health, and appetites to match, waiting for spring release. All four beavers grew up wild; all four encountered humans who could give lip service to the nobility of the beaver as a symbol of Canada, "but not in our backyard!"

A very sincere letter from a private school in Toronto — a school that prides itself on teaching the importance of the relationship between humans and the environment — said: "Thank you for being able to take the two beavers who had made their home in our pond. In the end, it was your Sanctuary which gave us the possibility of live-trapping; otherwise they would have had to be killed. We did not have the resources both to keep them and protect ourselves from the

On the way to freedom — a bit of a rough trip.

131

hazard of possibly having our road under water — a road which is also the only access to a senior's residence. We loved our beavers. It was so exciting that they came to us."

The person who wrote this letter really did care but was caught in an economic conflict. Several things could have been done, such as fencing or placing beaver bafflers in a culvert under the road to keep the beavers and let the children at the school watch, study and come to understand that the beaver is more than a rodent on a five-cent piece of money.

The other pair of beavers had been unwise enough to try to find a home in the stream running through an outdoor education center. Again, at the center there was one person who cared and phoned.

At first, I tried to be reasonable. "An outdoor education center? Beavers have moved in? What a chance to let the children watch and learn . . . ."

"But," came the patient reply, "they might cross the road and cut down the neighbor's trees, and they are millionaires and they might sue us."

A trapper had already been hired to kill the beavers, but our friend got there first, live-trapped the beavers and brought them to us. Knowing beavers, he also brought twenty bushels of apples.

Spring will come. These four beavers will be taken to a remote place in the wild, where, though away from human population, we will be able to monitor them. There they will take up their interrupted lives as free-living creatures. The children who could have learned so much will continue to read about them, look at pictures and learn to be as fearful as the adults who teach them.

Keeping records is one of the more tedious necessities of running a Sanctuary — very necessary for research, but also necessary to keep the government happy. As a result, I can look back over last year and be reminded that it began with the arrival of a fox (live-trapped because he was raiding a chicken coop), a moose calf that arrived dead because it died en route, a lion cub, several flying squirrels and, almost a year ago, Cody, the beaver. In March, April and May 1999 it was raccoons, rabbits, a bear cub from Quebec and a moose calf from Sudbury. And then, June 11, 1999, one beaver kit from Wildcare in Toronto. This kit became Casey, the bossy little beaver who is spending her first winter in our downstairs enclosure.

Casey was scarcely two weeks old, small, round and very hungry. Though I had been phoned and had certainly, willingly agreed to raise her, I was not expecting her so soon when, late one Friday night, I answered a knock at the door and was presented with a very hungry kit.

"They heard I was coming up this way," explained the young man who handed me the box holding the beaver, "so they asked me to drop it off."

The kit had been found washed up on the rocks along the shore of Lake Ontario, not far from the mouth of the Humber River. No one knew what had happened to separate her from her family, but she certainly needed help. And it was given. But more about that later.

JUNE 16, 1999: A beaver kit from Baysville! Cassidy!

Without a telephone, life at a Sanctuary would be very quiet. Even dull? This call was from Baysville, just the other side of Huntsville. Would I take care of a baby beaver? Since I would willingly circle the globe for a beaver, the trip to Baysville was no problem at all.

We found an elderly gentleman, white-haired (anybody's picture of the ideal grandfather), sitting on his porch in his rocking chair, holding a very small beaver wrapped in a towel and stroking it gently. Real Norman Rockwell stuff.

The elderly gentleman was a retired trapper. In his life, he had killed hundreds of beavers. (Is the human being the only animal capable of such contradictions?) Since then, I have sometimes wondered if that little beaver sensed more than we did. He is the only tiny beaver kit I have ever handled who absolutely refuses to trust any human. Perhaps his advent into our world was too catastrophic to be forgotten.

On one quiet spring day he had been with his family in the secure darkness of the lodge. How could that beaver family have known that cottagers, up from the city for the first time after the winter, would find the lodge offensive? This has been beaver country for centuries. But suddenly, the world erupted. The lodge was torn apart. His parents were trapped, his siblings shouted, frantically splashed. His entire family was hauled away. He was alone, small, frightened.

A great quietness surrounded him until the humans returned to discover that they had overlooked one kit. They caught him in a dip net. They thought him cute and tried to cuddle him. But they made no effort to return him to his family.

Instead, the little beaver we will name Cassidy will spend his kitten days with Casey.

As I have already indicated, the organs of a beaver are all internal, so short of an Xray, determining the gender of a beaver is somewhat difficult. Only another beaver instinctively knows for sure. One indication, which I think is reasonably valid, is that because the male is the major defender of territory, he is often the more aggressive. Since assigning sex on the basis of crankiness is manifestly politically incorrect, I assign gender merely as the beaver impresses me. I found myself referring to Casey as "she" and Cassidy as "he," even the real risk of being completely wrong being preferable to the depersonalization of "it."

Casey and Cassidy were given a lodge in the nursery in the barn, thick with straw and a water pan big enough to accommodate a baby beaver if, by any chance, he or she wanted to swim. Generally, very small beavers do not. For the first days they were warmed by a heat lamp hooked far enough above to give steady warmth without too much heat. They should have had a big, warm, soft mother beaver!

And for the first few days, like true beavers, they maintained a family distinction and slept at opposite ends of the box. But one morning I found them curled up together, a small mound of brown fur.

At first their formula (puppy Esbilac) was offered in a baby bottle. Casey would clasp the bottle in my hand to hold it steady while she suckled enthusiastically. Unless he was desperately hungry, Cassidy was reluctant to the point of refusal. Worried, I drenched brown bread in the Esbilac and offered it to him in a bowl. He could suck it up in privacy, and that was much more acceptable to him. Within a few days Casey, too, decided the bread method was a good idea, and I had no more beaver baby bottles to prepare. I missed it!

I began to offer them sliced yam (they liked it), apple (it was merely acceptable), clover, dandelion greens, wild raspberry cane and aspen leaves. The raspberry and aspen were favorites. I also began to find occasional teeth marks on the branches and knew they were beginning to be real beavers and gnawing!

I suppose beaver kits are like children; if you see them constantly, hour by hour, day after day, you do not particularly notice their gradual physical growth. Two months later, I was still under the impression that Casey and Cassidy were very small beavers. Actually, they had almost doubled in size! However, personalities remained constant. Casey was outgoing, chatty, friendly. Cassidy remained aloof, distrustful. We moved them to a larger outdoor cage, and I gave them a large pan of water, which, except for drinking, they continued to ignore. They had lots of straw for warmth, but they seemed to like the natural sunlight.

Casey I could take for walks. She trundled after me like a well-trained puppy. Cassidy resented even being touched. Finally, when enough raccoon babies had graduated to large enclosures, a large cage was available for the beavers. They had space, four feet by six feet, a pan big enough to swim in and lots of food, and since they showed no desire to be weaned, the heaping bowls of bread and formula continued. But the yams were no longer sliced. Raspberry cane and aspen came in larger bundles. Willow and some cattail roots were added to the diet. Casey started to push straw around, even carrying it in her mouth to make better beds, and they began to cover themselves with straw.

Most of their activity was at night. In the mornings, the food was gone, the water pan had been swum in and decorated with scat droppings, and the beavers were wet. Casey began demanding even more food; Cassidy, slightly behind her and more belligerent, waited. Their teeth had begun to turn orange.

AUGUST 15, 1999: Cory!

A busy visiting day: people everywhere. I was sitting on the veranda steps, discussing porcupines with some of the visitors, when the phone, lying beside me, rang. The voice on the other end of the line was masculine, grumpy and abrupt.

"Got another beaver. Want it?"

"Yes!" (Is there any other answer?)

He continued: "This year's kit. In my trap. Don't want it around here."

"We will come and get it right away," I replied, suddenly remembering this man. Once before, he had live trapped a large beaver who had committed the unpardonable sin of coming out of the river and eating the apples on the ground beneath his tree. Well, I struggled to give him credit — at least he was not killing them.

He went on to say, "Don't come until eight. Got a baptism going on here."

To which I answered, "Okay."

At eight o'clock, promptly, our white van wound down the narrow driveway to the little peninsula of land cutting into the winding river. The baptismal service seemed to be over, but shouting children were everywhere. Careful adults (and not one female in pants; somehow the adults looked as though they were living in a world of fifty years ago) looked at us, but apart from one or two hesitant smiles, no one spoke. I could not help wondering if the baptismal service had involved total immersion in the reedy river, and I think perhaps it had. I also wondered if that had been the reason the little beaver had not been welcome!

"Over there!" the elderly gentleman said, pointing beside a shed down at the shore. The trap, homemade, was contrived from a rusty tin barrel. I recognized it as the same trap that had held the big beaver several years ago. In its dark interior, the little beaver hunched in fear. When we tried to move him, his tail slapped in anger. Tony covered him with a net and transferred him to clean straw in a small kennel.

So Cory (that became his name) left the baptismal bay and was brought to a place where he could receive care. Just now, he is living in a cage pressed close against that of Casey and Cassidy. The introduction to his new family should be slow, but there is already a tentative acceptance. When a large pen is available, I will turn it into acceptable beaver habitat and put the three beavers together.

SEPTEMBER 12, 1999: The three beavers are all in one enclosure now, up by the barn. Harriette, a bear cub, graduated to the seven-acre enclosure back in the bush, leaving her big cage and large, hollow log (which has a natural window where, I presume, a branch had once been). The cage and log were thoroughly scrubbed, straw strewn around the floor. A flat water pool, easily large enough for a beaver to swim in, was installed and all was ready for the beavers. Cory's introduction caused no problems. He is a little bigger than the others and quite wary, but is eating well, cuddling into the log with the others and, when everything is quiet, coming out to swim.

SEPTEMBER 13, 1999: This morning when I went to visit, all three beavers were out of their log, even Cory. I put big branches of raspberry cane by the pond. They all munched away. And I used up a lot of film!

SEPTEMBER 18, 1999: A fourth, very angry young beaver, Carling, has come for the winter. A group of cottagers near Port Carling have decided that the beavers on "their" wetland must be eliminated. Only one young couple had the compassion and courage to protest. The neighbors want the beavers shot. The couple have managed to gain enough time for us to attempt to live-trap them.

We succeeded in catching two huge adults and released them into Quetico's pond. Today, we caught a kit. Because there is no way we can be sure that the large beavers are the parents of this particular kit (or even if they are parents), or that they would locate it in the wild, I do not think we should release him. Alone in the wild for its first winter, it would surely die. So we will try to integrate him with the other three.

SEPTEMBER 22, 1999: So far, Carling has not shown any desire to integrate. He is in the enclosure next to the others but is still afraid of them. Yesterday morning Tony thought that Carling had been at the fence watching the others, so he put Casey in with him. Carling immediately charged her, so he quickly removed her. Last night, though, I saw Carling and Cassidy nose to nose through the fence. Perhaps the union is only a matter of time. The live trap is still out in the wetland. I wish we could catch a sibling. I wonder if the cottagers there know or care about the distress they are causing one little creature.

SEPTEMBER 23, 1999: Tony lifted a corner of the fence so that if Carling wants to join the others he can. When I went out, Carling and Cory were together in the corner of his pen, while the other two were still in the log.

SEPTEMBER 24, 1999: Beavers are so territorial, yet so family oriented. I suppose the three were young enough when they were put together, but it seems we may have crossed some line. Today the three were together in their kennel. Carling was alone in the log. I put a big pile of raspberry cane and yams beside the log, hoping the food, very plentiful, would attract them together.

SEPTEMBER 25, 1999: They are still staying apart.

SEPTEMBER, 30, 1999: I found a large wound on the back of Carling's neck. It seems that one of the other three attacked. Tony closed the hole in the fence so they are now separated again.

OCTOBER 1, 1999: Carling died during the night.

Several weeks later, the young couple live-trapped one more kit. From the moment we looked into his kennel and his tail drummed in warning, we had a good idea of his temperament. We named him fireCracker.

Winter quarters for the young beavers are in the fieldstone basement of my house. The original pen, large and square, contains a bathtub, a kennel and lots of clean straw. Originally the pen was built of eight-inch logs. The theory was that such small beavers would not chisel their way through. Wrong! The logs are now covered with wire mesh. Right against the side of the first enclosure, a second enclosure stands ready. This seemed a good place for fireCracker.

Cracker lived up to his name splendidly. He spent a good deal of his time in his pond. If any human approached, he did not merely slap his tail or drum it, he exploded! The eruption of water was volcanic. Since we were never left in any doubt about his opinion of the human race, we arrived at a compromise. We would keep him warm, fed and his water clean. Perhaps, because he had not yet in his young life even experienced a winter, he did not properly value our commitment. But as his part of the deal, he was not to drown us.

Winter settled over the Sanctuary. All the creatures were cared for, most of them awaiting spring release. The beavers, all of them, content, quiet, eating well, and waiting.

On February 12, 2000, just around four-thirty, the telephone rang. I had been away from home for a few hours and, returning home, found that my dogs had pretty much totaled the house. Several books (including the telephone book), an antique hand mirror, a sheaf of drawings, a towel, a pair of warm woolen socks and a shoe were all strewn in tatters throughout the house. The dogs greeted me joyously. I put them out into their run, where they would have been all day if the weather had not been so cold. That was the point at which the phone rang. If I barked "Aspen Valley Wildlife Sanctuary" rather crossly into the phone, the young man at the other end was too polite to notice.

His question: "Do you take beavers?" (The dogs received instant forgiveness!) "Yes!" I replied.

"At least I think it is a beaver," he continued. "It's too big to be a muskrat. But its tail . . . ." His voice trailed away. "Tell me how to get to your place and we will bring it."

A three-hour drive? On a cold, cold winter night? This young man really cared. "I'll be waiting," I said. "Keep it warm."

Well after nine o'clock, his van pulled up to the house, and in a small wire cage in the back huddled the beaver. It was so thin that we could feel its backbone and its ribs, the pitiful remains of its tail half under, half looped around its meagre rump. What a horrible mess!

Tony made a bigger cage and filled it, deep and warm, with straw, water, an apple, yams, a carrot and a thick log of aspen. The beaver took a long drink and immediately began chiselling the bark from the aspen — a good sign.

This was our first beaver of the century — of the new millennium — and just now seemed to be a fearful echo of our experience exactly one year ago with Cody. Perhaps I am being naive, but oh, I do hope!

While government publications are still reporting, with keen enthusiasm, that our trappers are "harvesting" between one hundred and fifty and one hundred and eighty-four *thousand* beaver pelts a year, worth three to five million dollars to our economy, two young people drove for hours through winter darkness and snow to save the life of a single beaver.

FEBRUARY 14, 2000: Valentine's Day. I wish I could make all sorts of "yucky" comments about true love and the relationships beavers have to each other, but I won't.

This morning we took Clancy, our new beaver, in to the veterinarian. Yesterday, being Sunday, we only phoned about Clancy's condition, and were told to give him one cc of Longisil by injection. We tried, but the needles we had would not penetrate Clancy's tough skin. So we were the first people in the veterinarian's office this morning. All veterinarians should begin a new week, especially one beginning with Valentine's Day, by having to examine a frostbitten beaver!

Clancy is eating well — mostly aspen— and that's a good sign. He is also quite aggressive, another good sign. However, Tony was able to hold him still while the veterinarian examined the tail. The tail is alive and relatively unharmed to about three inches from the base. Then the horror begins. Frostbite is the most likely culprit, as though, caught in a trap, the tail broke there and the frantic beaver tried to chew himself free. Only the long bone down the middle, covered with what looks like chewed meat, remains. His hands also show abrasion, as though he had been scrambling.

They mentioned amputation, but a tail is so very important to a beaver. Only the last few inches seemed to be cold and therefore dead. We decided to treat for infection and to wait and see if that part would simply fall off; then as much of the tail as possible would be saved. Never mind what it would look like! Clancy had to have one-and-a-half cc's of Longisil every other day. We were given some bigger needles.

Clancy is now in a large wire cage in the warmth of the barn. He is nestled into deep, clean straw, has a pan of water, and aspen branches, yams, apples, carrots, and romaine lettuce. So far he just nibbles at our offerings, although he cleans aspen branches splendidly. We are hopeful. We also remember Cody . . . .

As I continue to contemplate the beavers we have had with us into the year 2000, let me tell you the next part in the story of those four beavers from the educational centers in the big city!

Over sixty years ago, as a child, I followed the adults down and up and down again on a trail through the bush to a small woodland lake. Back then, no road led to the lake, no cottages rimmed the shores. Wonderfully, at that lake the isolation still exists: a lake, an island, rocky shores, and at the far end, a swampy place where the water flows in — water that comes from spring-fed creeks and smaller lakes, all still largely untouched by humans.

A few weeks ago, I walked that trail again. This time, I was the older person, but again, following, was a small group of young people. They walked two by two, each pair carrying a cage, and in each cage a beaver on its way to freedom.

Huge, beautiful, wild beavers. They had not asked to be taken from the lodges where they had lived for years; they had not enjoyed the winter they had had to spend in our barn (though I think they would have to admit that the food was pretty good!), but they were alive and within minutes would be free again.

To those four beavers, the winter must have seemed very long. But they had large, warm enclosures, with ponds where they could enjoy some water. And lots of food (actually, if truth be told, feeding beavers costs us more than feeding our lion!): apples, yams, corn on the cob, romaine lettuce, and aspen branches. They ate, stayed healthy, and never showed the slightest interest in being friendly. Their fur gleamed. Their eyes were wary. I suppose they were wondering, in the unfamiliar darkness of a barn, what the future held for them.

It held a wonderful, remote lake in Muskoka. Over the long years, the trail into the lake had changed very little: tall pines, rocks, moss, quiet. As we arrived at the shore of the lake and the young people set down the kennels, the only sounds were still those of the water and the trees. We opened the doors of the kennels.

Hesitantly at first, and then rapidly, the beavers moved out, down the rocks and into the water. Clean, fresh, wild water. Smoothly the beavers swam, sliding under the surface and up again, out into the lake, under and up, swimming, stopping to drift a little, maybe wondering at the new world given to them.

And so we left them.

Maybe I am dreaming the impossible dream: Is it likely that the day will come soon when we humans will not merely tolerate beavers but will come to understand the huge contribution that they make to our environment?

CASEY THE CAREGIVER

The last chapter had been written; the book was finished, and then along came Casey — the caregiver. Casey has a story that must be told!

I had been contacted by a wildlife group in Toronto and asked if I would take on the care of a baby beaver. No problem. I know that taking the responsibility for a little beaver is at least a two-year commitment and am willing to commit my entire life to beavers. I wasn't told the actual time the beaver would be sent up to the Sanctuary and late that Friday night when a knock came on my door, I was already prepared for bed, quite unprepared for the arrival of the kit.

Casey was the first beaver kit of the 1999–2000 season. All the beavers who arrived during the year would have names beginning with the letter *C*. So, by the end of the season, we had Cassidy, Cory, Carling, fireCracker (usually called Cracker), Clancy and Carly.

From the beginning, Casey was a bossy little beaver. Her first companion was Cassidy, who arrived about ten days after she did. His past was partly known. Cottagers had arrived at their summer place to find a beaver lodge in the boathouse. A hired trapper had moved the beavers out to a more distant lake but missed one very small kit. Nobody was willing to take it out to its family, so it was sent here.

Cassidy was unwilling to take the bottle, unwilling to be handled. Very rightfully, he seemed to have a grudge against the human race. Casey was good to him, cuddling close and sharing the Esbilac-soaked bread with him, thus encouraging him to eat. In August they were joined by Cory, a beaver kit live trapped in Huntsville simply because the humans there did not want "those stupid beavers." Cassidy took it in her stride. After that came fireCracker, with his dangerous tail, live-trapped because humans wanted the wetland cleared so they could have a lawn.

Casey remained dominant. Eventually we had to separate Cassidy and fireCracker, but Casey managed to pacify the rest of her family. For the winter I had three kits in the downstairs enclosure — Casey, Cory and fireCracker. Cassidy was happy and alone in the warmth of the barn.

Casey was the most authentic "busy beaver" I have ever known. She literally helped me with the cleaning of their pen. When I started to rake together all the used straw, she would carry over armfuls and put them onto the pile. She pushed new, clean straw into the farthest corners. She stacked her peeled sticks around the kennel as though she were doing her best to make a lodge. Meanwhile, Cory was passive, while fireCracker continued to detonate at every approach.

One day I was in a hurry to get everything cleaned, but Cory and fireCracker were in the kennel and were, by then, certainly too big for

Casey as a kit.

me to argue with and dump out. So I shrugged, decided the situation was not all that critical, and left. I went back to my work upstairs, but, hearing a disturbance, returned quickly down. Casey had turfed the two bigger beavers out of the kennel, and they now sulked in the far corner of the enclosure. She had pushed out all the used straw and was heaping it in a corner, then began gathering clean straw and filling the kennel!

For the next several months, as winter began to give way to spring, Casey's life followed the normal course for beavers growing up in the Sanctuary. The three beavers became too big for the basement pen and were moved to a larger pen with a larger pond inside the barn. As the weather outside continued to grow warmer, we fixed up yet another pen outside the barn, against the old stone foundation. There, in a row of pens, the beavers would stay until the ice melted on the big beaver enclosure, when the beavers presently living there, Chinook and Tattertail, would go free.

The young beavers now had a hollow log for a lodge and a much larger pond. We brought them lots of aspen so that they could eat, build, and generally behave as beavers like to do. Almost immediately we had to erect a barrier along the fence between the pond and the passageway where humans walked, as Cracker felt it was necessary to warn the world away. The splash of his tail on the water was roughly equivalent to a brief, fierce thunderstorm. Cory went quietly about his way, neither as cranky as fireCracker nor as friendly as Casey.

Casey continued to be friendly and a little bit domineering over the other beavers. She would come to the gate to be talked to. She would come out so that she could be rubbed behind her ears and touched on her nose. And she would explore the passageway, but always returned to the pen with a minimum of coaxing.

One of the other beavers that arrived while Casey was with us was Clancy. About the middle of February the telephone rang yet again. "Do you take beavers?" I am afraid I always sound too eager and willing. This time I added, "How did you find a beaver in February?"

"It was sitting out beside the highway," he explained, and continued, "at least I think it's a beaver . . . ."

"Can't you tell by the tail?"

"No. But it is too big to be a muskrat. Wait until you see it."

The young man was calling from over near Peterborough, so the trip to the Sanctuary would take several hours. However, he cared enough about the beaver that he did bring it, through cold and snow and the almost dark evening. When we opened the kennel and saw the beaver — a large beaver — we could understand about the tail. It had been broken, most probably, like Cody's, in a trap, and frozen. Most of it had fallen away, all except the little strip of bone which could have been a rat's tail. This beaver became Clancy.

Clancy made fireCracker look good-tempered. We made him a warm pen in the barn, gave him shots to prevent infection, and fed him. But he was too angry to eat.

The bone finally fell away, but the stump of the tail healed well. He is very able and swims just fine. His only handicap is that he cannot smack the tail he no longer has. He will eventually go free.

The change in Casey's story did not begin with a phone call. A van simply came up the laneway, and a couple who knew we loved beavers got out. They did not hesitate. They opened the back doors of the van, and there, in a cage, was another beaver lying quietly — too quietly.

"She was picked up beside the road," they explained. "She had been hit by a car. We don't know if anything can be done . . . ."

We did not know either. She was paralyzed from the waist back — her great webbed feet trailing out behind, her tail hanging motionless.

"We had her Xrayed," they added, "and no bones are broken."

We made the pen next to the other beavers as comfortable as we could, with a hollow log, lots of warm straw and a pond. We laid her down in the straw. She made no attempt to move. Seeing her so inert, someone said, "There is no hope that she can survive and ever walk or swim again. It would probably be better to have her euthanized."

Curiously, Casey came to the separating fence and looked through. She thought otherwise!

Like the other beavers already mentioned in this book, Casey had evidently not read any biology books about beavers. She didn't know that she was not supposed to accept another beaver from outside her own family, at least not at her age. Carly (as we named the beaver) slept against the fence, and Casey began to sleep as close as she could beside

147

her. Casey started to poke food through the fence — aspen, apple, yam, and bits of bread. Carly began to eat and eat well.

Cracker and Cory ignored the situation. Spring grew warm, and Chinook and Tattertail were set free. Cracker and Cory, being much larger than Casey, were taken to a place out in the wild (on our property, where we could monitor them) and given their freedom. We moved Casey in with Carly.

Casey was now free to begin her nursing in earnest. She pushed at Carly. She tried to make Carly follow her, and poor Carly, willingly enough, dragged herself along, feet and tail trailing limply. Once she even managed to pull herself into the log. I sat with her every day and massaged her hips and legs, a method that had enabled several skunks paralyzed in the same way to walk again; however, I saw no improvement.

We had moved Clancy down to the pond enclosure. Tail or no tail, he was doing well, so we decided that Casey and Carly would be moved down there, too. The pond is large enough and deep enough to allow the beavers a good chance to swim. Previous occupants had built a lodge and had tunneled under the banks so that a network of canals exists. The only other occupant is a large, blind skunk named Amos. He's not bothered by any of the beavers.

Water therapy is sometimes used to treat paralysis. When swimming, a beaver's front hands are tucked up against its chest; the powerful, webbed back feet are used to propel it through the water. The tail acts as a rudder, also providing the thrust when the beaver wants to dive. On land, when a beaver rises to its hind feet, the tail is used for balance. With Carly's extensive paralysis, how safe would it be to commit her to the pond? What future did she have if she were to remain paralyzed? Enter Casey, again!

We moved the beavers to the big enclosure. Immediately, Casey was in the water. She had never known so much water and such deep water. Around and around she swam, slipping under the surface,

*Casey and Clancy enjoying the first warm spring sunshine
at the entrance to their lodge.*

coming up and climbing out on the bank to groom herself, but only for
a moment, because she wanted to swim.

Carefully, we lowered Carly into the water. She remained motionless, only her head above the surface. We were taking a real chance!
However, Casey swam over, circled her, and began nudging her out
into the pond. We could do nothing more than leave them there
together.

Carly disappeared. For the next few days when I took the food into
the enclosure, Casey came up the bank. Clancy circled in the water
until I left, then he came to take his share. In the late afternoons, I put
apples and yams into the water where they would be available to Carly.
Always, in the morning, all the food had disappeared. Still, I worried.

Had Carly gotten herself caught in one of the caves or tunnels? Was she starving? And what could I do if she was?

One evening, I heard a beaver conversation carried on with some vigour in the cave on the far shore — a good sign! After several days Carly reappeared, swimming, with Casey always beside her, behind her, helping. Carly's whole body was level with the water (her back feet must have strength!), but the tail still appeared to drag. She was thin; I could see her hip bones, and, I thought, just possibly movement. Casey often swam with her. They circled, touched noses, and dived — two young beavers at play. Almost normal play.

Two afternoons a week we allow visitors to the Sanctuary. Casey began to enjoy the attention. As the living symbol of Canada, she fascinated visitors from Europe, allowing children to put their fingers through the fence and touch a real beaver. Occasionally, Carly would drag herself to the fence, more to be with Casey than to visit with the humans. She still did not really trust anyone.

I had no idea how Casey decided who was to be trusted and who was not. At one point a well-known photographer traveled to the Sanctuary from Toronto. He wanted pictures of wolves. Our wolves co-operated, even howling in the true stereotype of howling. He also managed to take some very good pictures of the big black bear. But he wanted pictures of beaver.

Though the beavers rarely appeared until late afternoon, yams usually sufficed as a bribe to make Casey, at least, come out. I took several yams into the enclosure, the photographer, camera ready, standing just behind. I called Casey and tossed one yam into the water so she would hear the splash. No action. We waited quite a while. Finally I saw the water quake a little, a sign of beaver movement in the cave, and then the trail of small bubbles on the surface. So quickly that the photographer had no time even to raise his camera, Casey grabbed the yam and disappeared. We saw the trail of bubbles back to the cave, heard a little beaver conversation, and that was it. No more beavers. No pictures.

In contrast, the day before, a columnist from the newspaper in Fergus had visited, not because he wanted anything in particular, he simply likes animals. Together, we went into the beaver enclosure, and I called Casey. Up the bank she came, no bribery necessary. She ignored me, approaching Peter's feet. She stretched up to see him. He knelt and talked to her; she didn't draw back. Peter was fascinated, remarking, "I have never touched a beaver before!"

So, on visiting day Casey sometimes appeared and sometimes she did not. On one particular and very special day at the Sanctuary, the visitors lingered long after our closing time. I began the evening feeding, taking my bucket of food into the enclosure. Casey, still talking to the humans beside the fence, ignored me.

A beaver came walking up the bank. Walking! A beaver with a tail. Not Clancy. An unexpected beaver. All four feet moving. Carly!

Presently, Casey came over, then she and Carly swam around and around in the pool. When the time comes, they will be released — together.

Norbert.

Epilogue

You have met my friends Swampy and Beaver and Quibble, who were the first teachers at the Sanctuary. Since then, so many beavers have passed through and gone on to be released into the wild to live natural lives. Some of them — Quetico, Tattertail and Chinook — have happy stories. Carling and Cody . . . we, as humans, owe them. We caused their suffering and their deaths. For them, and a million more like them, we must make our wilderness and our world a better place. Could we ever convince a tailless beaver, like Clancy, that humans are trustworthy?

Right now our smallest beaver is a three-month-old kit named Norbert. He is a little brown bundle of quivering anger. A few weeks ago, he was brought to us from an island in Georgian Bay. Somehow, very small and alone, he had escaped the massacre of his entire family. Someone shot them because they were "nuisance" beavers.

When I speak, I want the audience to know the wonder of animals. I share stories of raccoons and foxes, of wolves and bears, stories to make the audience sometimes laugh and sometimes cry. And of course I tell stories about beavers. I talk to the humans about the world we should be sharing with these creatures, the privilege of sharing and the value of their friendship. Such talks can be interesting and pleasant, but I will not forget the pledge I made to Cody.

Trapping, we are told, is an important industry, supported by our government. Millions of beavers have died unecessarily. And they still do. Humane traps? This is the kind of trap sanctioned by the Canadian taxpayer. The following description is not mine, but that of a trapper who explained how humane the traps are!

"A Conibear Trap is a steel, ten-inch-square spring mechanism that is buried in underwater runways in the dam and which snaps shut when the beaver noses into a release trigger. Either the animal's skull is crushed, or the third vertebrae, at the neck, is broken. It is considered an instant kill."

What a myth! Tell any human that having one's skull crushed or neck broken is humane.

A conservation officer who was consulted by the *Kingston Whig Standard* in August 1986, stated that "at the age of two, beavers are evicted from the home lodge, and must find abodes elsewhere. If they come back, the parents eat them." This, another myth, is complete and utter nonsense, and also rather alarming — if readers actually believed it!

Imagine a land with no beavers, with no ponds in the woods and fields, no place for the ducks or geese or the frogs, no place for the deer and moose, the raccoons and skunks and foxes and muskrats and . . . the list is without end. All our wilderness depends on the water the beaver stores.

A headline from the *New York Times*, many years ago, underscores the importance of beavers in relationship to water: "U.S. Keeps Beaver Busy Restoring Creeks." Another headline, from a few years later, reads, "Town Thanks Beavers for Water During Drought."

This, more recently, in the *London Free Press*, August 2000, entitled, "Beavers Work Holding:"

Madoc: "Beavers are the only thing preventing a possible environmental disaster on the Moira River in Eastern Ontario," area residents are being told. Government officials have warned about forty local residents and cottagers that there is no back-up plan to stop the spread of arsenic and heavy metal contamination from sediment if the beaver dams in Young's Creek break.

A glimmer of hope? We're working on it, Cody!

Canadian artist John Doherty has a cottage in Muskoka where he and his family spend long, warm summer days. John's work fits no classification — it is simply unique and rather wonderful. The physical characteristics of his animals could not be captured by any camera. No abstraction could express the soul, the spirit that animates his wolves, his bears, his humans, his otters. He paints on antlers and bones, on drums and on paddles, not because tourists might consider such items quaint, but because through the painting, some piece of the wilderness remains in the skull or the feather or the claw and speaks out as it did in life. The wolves he paints are wild and free; his otters laugh; his humans are one with the wild things.

The Dohertys are frequent visitors to the Sanctuary and loyal supporters. Over the years, when he has visited, I have complained to John that Canadian artists seldom portray beavers. One finds beavers on our currency (the five-cent piece), on the coat of arms and in advertising, but not much more. One time John smiled and presented me with a paddle, on which, in a tumbling cascade of water, otters play. I loved the paddle, but I continued to complain. "Beavers, please," I said.

At about that time, Richard and Lynda Moxley, friends of the Sanctuary who work closely with Native people in Toronto, presented me with a medicine drum. Made of wood and moose hide, the drum's voice was meant to be heard in this world and the other.

"It should have a symbol or design on it," Richard commented.

I thought of John. Although John is not Native, the earth has a soul that recognizes those who love her and the mystery that is at her heart. So I gave the drum to John. "Beavers," I requested. He laughed!

Summer, fall, and the long, long winter passed. I did not see any of the Doherty family. Sometimes I wondered about the drum, but life was busy with creatures arriving and needing care.

A beaver found injured on the 401 Highway
enjoys the quiet of the sanctuary pond. He recovered and went free.

Quibble was showing his age. He moved more slowly, ate less, slept deeply. Every part of me was protesting, "Don't grow old — don't die!" Then spring came and he was in his outdoor enclosure. He swam sometimes, slowly. He slept in the warm sunshine. Then one day he did not wake up.

Only a few days later, John returned with the drum. "I could not get going on it," he said, "until the last few days." He handed me the medicine drum. A beaver, of course. But not just any beaver. It was Quibble.

A large, crimson moon, from which emanate fine rays, almost like the spray of a waterfall, spread over the rim of a ghostly white forest and beaver pond, with a distant lodge. A beaver, content and peaceful, nibbles aspen leaves. Not just any beaver. Quibble.

Below the surface of the water is another beaver, transparent, so that we see his spirit. The soul of all beavers. The certainty of life everlasting.

My concept of eternity does not consist of lots of cherubims and seraphim and angry angels flying around with blaring trumpets. I think that heaven encompasses an infinite curve of wetlands in wide valleys, stretching on and on, where wildlife, all interdependent, live at last in peace. There I will find the beavers, those who have been my friends, working away. They would not be content or happy if they were not working! All of them, from that first, somewhat shadowy Ah-mik, to the angry Norbert, who is living here now, growing, waiting to be free.